Backstories of Chaos,
Rescue & Worship

OH-NO AHA and GLORY BE

MATT TULLOS
Illustrated by Travis Foster

Published by Innovo Publishing, LLC
www.innovopublishing.com
1-888-546-2111

Publishing Books, eBooks, Audiobooks, Music, Screenplays, & Courses
For the Christian & Wholesome Markets

OH-NO, AHA, AND GLORY BE
Backstories of Chaos, Rescue & Worship

Copyright © 2023 by Matt Tullos
All rights reserved.
onaha.com

No part of this publication may be reproduced, stored in a retrieval system, or transmitted in any form or by any means electronic, mechanical, photocopying, recording, or otherwise, without the prior written permission of the Author.

Some names referenced in this book were changed to protect the identity of the individual.

Unless otherwise noted, all scripture is taken from the Christian Standard Bible. Copyright © 2017 by Holman Bible Publishers. Used by permission. Christian Standard Bible®, and CSB® are federally registered trademarks of Holman Bible Publishers, all rights reserved.

Scripture marked HCSB is taken from the Holman Christian Standard Bible (HCSB). Copyright © 1999, 2000, 2002, 2003, 2009 by Holman Bible Publishers, Nashville Tennessee. All rights reserved.

Library of Congress Control Number: 2023906055
ISBN: 978-1-61314-912-6

Cover Design & Interior Layout: Innovo Publishing, LLC
Cover and Interior Illustrations: Travis Foster

Printed in the United States of America
U.S. Printing History
First Edition: 2023

Has God called you to create a Christian or wholesome book, eBook, audiobook, music album, screenplay, or curricula? Visit Innovo Publishing or our educational center cpportal.com to learn how to accomplish your calling with excellence.

Dedication

This little book is dedicated to the stumblers, the scattered, the seekers, and the sojourners. It's dedicated to the losers—those beautiful, irresistible people who lose their dignity, their pride, their shoulder chips, and their keys from time to time. It's dedicated to the underdogs, the anxious, the third stringers, and the overachievers. It's for the dreamers who have lost touch with reality. It's dedicated to the practical who haven't dreamed in years. It's for those who have walked with God for fifty years as well as those who haven't taken one step toward Him. It's for the holy and the humiliated, the righteous and the restless, the vain and the virtuous. I suppose, if you are breathing, it's dedicated to you.

I know what you're thinking, and you're right: this dedication is not very discriminating. It's quite unfocused, far-reaching, and confounding. Well, if you're baffled by my list, you should see God's. If you've ever epically faceplanted on the dancefloor of life, you're thankful for a God who equates elitism with immorality. You thank God for His list.

So there's that.

This book—dear and gracious reader, my new best friend—is dedicated to you.

Contents

Dedication 5
Contents 7
Introduction 9

Part 1:
All Glory Be 11

Part 2:
Marriage 43

Part 3:
Parenting 67

Part 4:
Church 125

Part 5:
Random Observations 139

Acknowledgments 173

Introduction

Last Thanksgiving my wife was in the kitchen with our sons and their girlfriends, preparing the traditional meal with the real napkins and fancy silverware. Somehow, as it often does when there are too many cooks in the kitchen, something went haywire. The paper towels next to the gas stove somehow burst into flames. One of my sons tossed it across the kitchen into the trash, and my wife, Darlene, dashed to the trash can because she feared that all the trash would go up into flames. The only problem with that action was that the dishwasher door was down, and she tripped, flying through the air. Like most accidents, everything turned to slow motion as I saw our thirty-seven years of marriage flash before my very eyes. We could have had a viral video on our hands if someone had the foresight to record it. The fire petered out as my wife miraculously landed on our unfortunate golden retriever who had innocently meandered into the kitchen looking for discarded giblets. The kitchen went from sheer panic to great calm to laughter. What a miraculous turn of events! They could have burned our house down and left my wife in a neck brace to say the least.

I believe most of our reactions to life's sudden twists and hair-pin turns could be categorized in three exclamatory statements: *Oh-No, Aha,* or *Glory Be*. These experiences, great and small, allow us the opportunity to engage, to mourn, to laugh, and to celebrate.

On this Thanksgiving, the "Oh-No" was the fire, the "Aha" was my son's quick and unwarranted idea to throw the flaming roll of paper towels in the trash, and the "Glory Be" was our overweight, unsuspecting golden retriever that unwittingly provided a soft landing space to break Darlene's fall. Life is filled with these sudden crises and unimaginable rescues. Some days we say, "Oh-No," some days we exclaim, "Aha," and almost every day, we say, "Glory Be!" And on rare occasions we say all of them in a minute. This is the nature of life and its symphony of sudden calamities and miraculous rescues.

> *Oh-No!*
> *Aha!*
> *&*
> *Glory Be!*

It's a pattern we see throughout the Bible:

> *Oh-No:* We just left Egypt, but they are chasing us down!
> *Aha:* Moses raises his arms with rod in hand, and God splits the water.
> *Glory Be:* Mariam leads worship as Israel does a victory dance to God.

Oh-No, Aha, and Glory Be

Oh-No: We need to get our friend to Jesus so he can be healed. But we can't get him to Jesus because all the Christ-followers are standing in the way!
Aha: Let's make a hole in the roof.
Glory Be: Jesus heals! He can walk! We've never seen anything like that before!

As you read scripture, I challenge you to look to notice the *Oh-No* (also known as *chaos*), the *Aha* (also known as *rescue*), and the *Glory Be* (also known as *worship*). They're everywhere.

This book is a celebration of these three exclamations. You'll read things written through my journey in the 90s, 00s, 10s, and 20s. I write this so that you don't believe that I still have toddlers. That would be the supreme *Oh-No*. Even though most of the stories are personal to me, I imagine they'll prompt memories and stories that are uniquely yours.

Note: This book is not progressive. It's a gumbo of memories, thoughts, and anecdotes. If you want to start from the back, be my guest. It's gloriously random that way.

PART 1:
All Glory Be

Oh-No: My eyes aren't on Jesus because I'm so busy.
Aha: Maybe I'm so busy because my eyes aren't on Jesus.
Glory Be: He's always got His eyes on me.

When I'm in a dark place, Jesus doesn't just sympathize and say, *Wow, that's got to be tough*. I can sense Him driving me back into His story and saying, *I know how you feel.* And that, my brothers and sisters, is good news.

I Can Even Use *That* Guy

Aren't you thankful that God didn't candy coat the chaotic journey of men in the Bible? We're easily intimidated by guys who seem to glide through life with little mess—a perfect backyard, six-pack abs, and a white-hot marriage. Instead, God gives us a book that reminds us on every page that He uses men who are still trying to figure things out. When I have one of those *man-what-was-I-thinking* moments, I remember Abraham who actually said to Pharaoh about his wife, "No, she's not my wife. She's uh . . . my sister. Yeah, that's it! My sister!"

When I think about my embarrassing, trip-over-my-own-feet-to-save-my-integrity moments, I think about Joseph who, when propositioned by Potiphar's wife, admirably ran away so fast he literally lost his clothes. We celebrate his virtue, but we have to agree that he needed a better belt.

Eutychus must be thanking God that there wasn't YouTube in the first century because a video of him falling out of a three-story building during Paul's Bible study in Acts 20 would have gone viral.

One universal truth of man is that we've all missed a rung, slept during worship, and said some epically stupid things at the exact time we shouldn't have. The mic was on, the occasion was not apropos, our judgment was obscured, or we just plain blew it. Period.

But it's all there in the Bible, and God manages to get the glory and make something amazing despite all the kooky conundrums we manufacture in our spare time. This is the book I love because it makes me feel like God could actually use an enigmatic, flawed, perplexing man like me. If fact, the Bible hints to the fact that He not only works with people like us, but He kind of enjoys telling the story. It's almost like He's saying, *Look at this! I can even use* that *guy!*

And you too may say, *There are many reasons why God shouldn't use me*. You're right! But don't worry. You're in good company.

Moses stuttered.
David's armor didn't fit.
John Mark was rejected by Paul.
Timothy had ulcers.
Hosea's wife was a prostitute.
Amos's only training was in the school of fig tree pruning.
Jacob was a liar.
David had an affair.

Solomon was too rich.
Jesus was too poor.
Abraham was too old.
David was too young.
Peter was afraid of death.
Lazarus was dead? Well, he was dead.
John was self-righteous.
Naomi was a widow.
Paul was a murderer.
So was Moses.
Jonah ran from God.
Miriam was a gossip.
Gideon and Thomas both doubted.
Jeremiah was depressed and suicidal.
Elijah was burned out.
John the Baptist was a loudmouth.
Martha was a worry-wart.
Mary was lazy.
Samson had long hair.
Noah got drunk.
Did I mention that Moses had a short fuse?
So did Peter, Paul—well, lots of folks did.

Aha Moment

"Now we have this treasure in clay jars, so that this extraordinary power may be from God and not from us."

(2 Corinthians 4:7)

But God doesn't require a job interview. He doesn't hire and fire like most bosses because He's more our Dad than our Boss. He doesn't look at financial gain or loss. He's not prejudiced or partial, not judging, grudging, sassy, or brassy, not deaf to our cry, not blind to our need. As much as we try, God's gifts are free. We could do wonderful things for wonderful people and still not be wonderful. Satan says, *You're not worthy.* Jesus says, *So what? Sit down! I am.* Satan looks back and sees our mistakes. God looks back and sees the cross. He doesn't calculate what you did in '98. It's not even on the record. Sure. There are lots of reasons why God shouldn't use me or you. But if you are magically in love with Him, if you hunger for Him more than your next breath, He'll use you in spite of who you are, where you've been, or what you look like. I pray that we will step out of our limitations into the unlimitable nature of who God is. Then our passion for God and our passion to communicate with Him will make mincemeat of our limitations.

Oh-no, Aha, and Glory Be

Matt Tullos

Goofy, Flawed, Yet Strangely Effective Prayers

Prayer mystifies, astounds, and enlivens me. Just to think that the same God that gave Jupiter rings actually has time to listen to what I have to say endows a sort of awe when I pray. He's actually interested in the details of my life while still having time to do all the big stuff. He can do what all mortal men and a handful of women can't: multitask. He is the master multitasker. Just the fact that He would be interested . . . wow. And I have said some fairly weird things, and I'm sure you have also.

I remember once I was praying in a group before we left on a mission trip, and I actually concluded the prayer before we left with a thoughtless, "Thank You, God. In Jesus's name, bye-bye." You don't live that one down. All the way to Guatemala and back, the mission team couldn't get over it. "In Jesus's name, bye-bye."

It's really painful to be scolded during a prayer. My ten-year-old son once prayed, "Lord, help my dad with his attitude. He's a grouch today." Yes, that's what I'd call an honest intercession and a stinging lateral rebuke.

Announcement prayers perplex me at church. "Lord, thank You for what You are going to do at the ladies event Friday night, the fifteenth at 6 p.m. Help us invite a friend and bring cookies for the annual cookie exchange. I also pray that they'll RSVP by Wednesday. That would be awesome. We hope you'll be there—I mean, I hope the ladies will be there."

There is a prayer I've prayed often during my life. Usually these prayers have something to do with a car. Occasions include when the minivan was hydroplaning or when my sixteen-year-old was driving or when my four-year-old somehow got in our car and shifted into neutral on a hill during a family picnic. It's a one-word prayer. I bet you've prayed it before. It's a loud prayer that God seems to always answer, and it goes something like this: *Arhhhhhhhhhhhhhh!* (Note: it usually lasts around fifteen seconds, and it works every time because miraculously nobody has ever been rushed to the hospital after I've prayed it.)

One of the oldest prayers of Christianity that is top of mind and tip of tongue through every season is a simple one: *Lord Jesus Christ, Son of God, have mercy.* Unlike many other prayers, I can say this in two point five seconds, which is about all the time I have in the middle of sudden emergencies. And it's one that He's always answered.

Thanks, Father. Bye-bye . . . I mean, amen.

Oh-No Admonition

"Rejoice always, pray constantly, give thanks in everything; for this is God's will for you in Christ Jesus."
(1 Thessalonians 5:16-18)

Aha Moment

"Hear my prayer, Lord, and listen to my cry for help; do not be silent at my tears. For I am here with you as an alien, a temporary resident like all my ancestors."
(Psalm 39:12)

Fear of Aunts

As a child, I grew up as a concrete thinker. Honestly, most of us were. That's just a fact about kids. They think concretely and are unable to process the subtle imagery adults use.

I remember I had a deep fear of Aunt Bonnie who told me that I was so cute she could just eat me up. I didn't understand and ran away in fear. All I knew was that my aunt was a cannibal, and I was spending a weekend at her house. Trauma.

It just seemed like my aunt said things that were strangely macabre. *Who is this woman? Is she really my aunt? How many children has she eaten?*

"Come here, Sugar. Let me wipe your face off."

"Wipe my face off? No!"

She thought I was being stubborn, but who in their right mind wipes someone's face completely OFF? There must be a law, an ordinance that would prohibit such a disfigurement. How would one see? How would one breathe?

I was often called a "toe-head." I still don't know what that referred to, but I spent more than one night performing a thorough inspection of my skull to make sure an eleventh toe wasn't about to burst forth from my temple. That's not the way I wanted to join the circus.

Later in life, we learn the difference between hyperbole and reality.

It took me a while to understand the concept of Jesus living inside me, dying to self, following Jesus, and giving Him everything. These aren't just overblown colloquialisms. These gigantic expressions are a mandate, especially for dads. There is nothing more important than letting these phrases become a reality, as we love our church, our family, and our friends.

I don't want people to look back at my life and say, *Sure, he talked about dying to himself, but that was just an exaggeration. He didn't mean that literally.* I don't want my kids to say, *Oh, when he talked about following Jesus, he didn't really mean* actually following *Jesus. He just meant that he admired the Man and thought he'd try to live a little like Him."*

I want them to say, *He really believed all that stuff about Jesus, and he was continually on a hunt for Him. He was obsessed with the fact that Jesus really rose from the dead.* I'd love it to be said of me after I die, *That crazy old dude actually prayed like Jesus could actually hear him.*

That's what would make me smile. And it's something that no one will wipe off my face.

Glory Be Declaration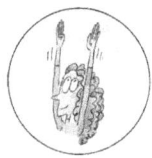

"I pursue as my goal the prize promised by God's heavenly call in Christ Jesus."

(Philippians 3:14)

A Tale of Two Dogs

Arthur and Frank were two of many family dogs that wound up at our place, but they both embraced vastly different worldviews. Frank was our conflicted dachshund. He was a feisty weeny dog that never met a stranger he liked. He was adorable but always up for escape. Chasing Frank reminded me of a bad episode of *Cops* where the suspects sprint through the alleys and over the hedges, narrowly escaping the long arm of the law. He would elude our grasp for minutes if not hours. Who needs a treadmill to stay in shape when you're doing daily wind sprints to capture Frank? Escape was his goal in life. Escape to where? I don't think any of us figured *that* out. I built a fence so that he could have just a taste of the outdoors. What was I thinking? It took me several afternoons, but like Houdini, Frank devised and mastered an escape strategy in under two minutes. Frank could have really used some pharmaceutical assistance, but I wasn't going to shell out the money for a dog shrink. The best I could tell, he was adopted into a loving home where there was plenty of food and fresh water, but the wide world of danger and vicarious survival called his name. He ended up where all our failed pets would go: the grandparents in rural Louisiana.

We discovered Arthur about a year later at a local dog pound. He had his faults, but one thing he never wanted to do was to go anywhere without us. We'd leave the door wide open, and he would wait for us to make the first move. We rarely even used a leash. Arthur was joined at the hip to our boys. He had no interest in going places without us. He would mourn our departure and celebrate our return. We gave him the freedom to go anywhere in the world, but his favorite place was with his people.

These two dogs serve as two distinct life strategies. There are some people, like Frank, who want nothing more than to climb over the boundaries of God's protection. Others are "*Arthur people*": they could go anywhere but are satisfied to be where they are loved the most.

I have to confess, in my younger years, I yearned to jump fences, sneak away, or burrow under God's gracious boundaries. I looked at every wall as a punishment and every rule as a burden to be cast aside. However, experience has taught me that there's no place like home, especially for an old mutt like me.

Oh-No Admonition

"Let us, then, make every effort to enter that rest, so that no one will fall into the same pattern of disobedience."

(Hebrews 4:11)

Matt Tullos

The Septic Week

Stuff like this usually happens before church. Darlene started the dishwasher, and I heard the eerie sound of rushing water downstairs. Knowing that we didn't have a decorative water fountain as the centerpiece of the man cave, I knew something was up. Our toilet downstairs transformed itself into a geyser, spewing filth like the volcanic eruptions of Mordor. It wasn't the kind of water anyone would want on the ceramic tile.

I went into high gear, rushing around bailing water, killing the dishwasher rinse cycle, and screaming for help. This began our ten days in septic purgatory. There were complications. We were renting the house after our last move, so we were dealing with lots of middlemen: the rental company, the warranty company, the plumbing company, the septic company, and last but not least, the gas company. The story's too long to describe in graphic detail. Suffice it to say that we all (including the owners of the house) were unaware that there were two, yes two, septic tanks, and one of the septic tanks had not been serviced in the home's twelve-year lifespan. That's a lot of . . . well . . . septic stuff. You know, the stuff that—this is awkward. The septic guys had to dig up the second septic tank, which was just below a gas line. That's how the gas company got involved. See, I wasn't just trying to be funny. The gas company really was involved.

I digress. I find a metaphor in the middle of all of this mess. We have our own emotional septic tanks for anger, frustration, fear, and disconnection. The trouble is, we rarely dig deep enough to get to the source of it all, and when we least expect it, there's sewage in the man cave—an emotional septic tank that overflows into our homes makes everything around us stink. So let's do the hard work of getting rid of all the mess so we can be the people God created us to be.

Aha Moment

"Let all bitterness, anger and wrath, shouting and slander be removed from you, along with all malice."

(Ephesians 4:3)

You Give Them Something

On a Sunday morning in my small church, I walked into the worship center, and the youth minister pulled me aside and said, "Pastor Bob had a little emergency with his mom and dad in Toledo. He flew out last night, and he asked me to preach, but it's been a crazy week and I'm totally gassed. Would you mind preaching?" The pre-service music had already started, and we were thirty seconds before the first song. He didn't wait for a response. He just walked up on stage to do the welcome.

I was a little woozy. I had to sit down. I whispered to my wife, Darlene, "I have absolutely no idea what I'm going to do. He didn't even wait for an answer." I can speak, but I'm kind of a planner. Should I just say, *We're just going to worship, take up the offering, and pray?* I flopped my Bible open in the seat next to me. This fortune cookie approach to getting a word from God rarely works. Jesus speaks from intentional study, not just flopping the Bible open and reading the first thing. I tried that once during a difficult day with Darlene, and the red letter verse I read was, "Woman, why are you crying?" I didn't try to work that into the situation. But this time, the first red letter words my eyes landed on were these: "You give them something to eat."

It was from the story of Jesus feeding the five thousand. The disciples were trying to get Jesus to make a public announcement that the multitude should go back home because the show was over, and they didn't have a fish and chips stand within ten square miles of the deserted place. But Jesus, the Creator of the universe, said casually to the disciples, "*You* give them something to eat."

That Sunday, I saw spiritually hungry people settling in for worship, and I had the spiritual equivalent of two eggs, a box of macaroni, a can of beans, and a three-year-old can of sardines. Lots of times I've heard Jesus whisper, *You give them something.* Why would an all-powerful God ask that of me? There are far better solutions out there! He wouldn't leave well enough alone. *You give them something.* In these moments, I do what we all do when Jesus asks and we say "yes": I start looking for scraps of something to use, things I forgot that I had, crazy ideas, and risky moves that I'm hesitant to try. I offer it. He takes it. He blesses it. And amazing stuff happens. Here's the thing: What I have is not extraordinary. Quite the opposite. It's not extraordinary until He gets His hands on it. It's just how the whole thing works. He wants to involve us in the process. It's all Him, but we get to come along for the ride.

He does this all the time. Jesus whispers to the disorganized mom, the introverted hostess, the stuttering leader, the guy with a sketchy past, the penniless widow, the uneducated mentor, the overwhelmed dad, and the inexperienced coach, *You give them something.* Perhaps because when these people succeed, there will be someone saying, *If God could use that person, there must be something to this thing they call gospel.*

Aha Moment

"Preach the word; be ready in season and out of season; correct, rebuke, and encourage with great patience and teaching."

(2 Timothy 4:2)

The Whac-a-Mole Days

Figuratively speaking, I love the *waterslide days*. Exciting, refreshing, and fun. On the *waterslide days*, you really don't have to do anything but lean back and let the giant-sized plumbing pipe do the rest. *Waterslide days* all end up in the predictable pool at the end of the tube. But more than I'd like, life is a game of *Whac-a-Mole*. You are at the noisy pizza place with a velvet coated hammer, whacking as fast as you can at the pesky little problems that pop up in a split second. For me, these are the days and sometimes weeks when my neat, predictable, iPhone friendly, Southern Living inspired, Billy Graham sounding persona is blown to smithereens.

Welcome to the *Whac-a-Mole days*. These are the days when projectile vomiting from the six-month-old intersects with the timing chain going out on the minivan while the eight-year-old gets called to the principal's office for throwing his yo-yo into the chili pot, causing second-degree burns to the lunchroom lady. It all comes in at once, and if you didn't have your coffee, quiet time, and morning kiss before it all went down, you'd probably be practicing macramé at the rehab center across town. There are days when the faster you whack the more the furry moles pop up from the game booth.

This is life in all its aspects. Not all days are *Whac-a-Mole days*, but we can rest assured that all winning streaks must come to an end, often with tumultuous crescendos when we least expect it. Surviving *Whac-a-Mole days* requires the heart of a Father who saw His share of rebelling children, deceptive villains, and dramatic teen romance disasters. I'm so glad that the Bible didn't leave out the *Whac-a-Mole days*. God left it all in a book for those messy days *we'd* experience from time to time.

King David, the man after God's own heart, survived a number of *Whac-a-Mole days*. There were days when he was surrounded, his family was kidnapped, his friends would turn on him, and his enemies would ramp up their attacks. I love the narrative of one of those days in 1 Samuel 30. Everything closed in on him and *"David encouraged himself in the Lord."* When there is no encouragement on the way from our friends, spouse, associates, or even the dog, we've got to learn how to do this. We've got to dig deep, splash cold water in our face, look ourselves in the mirror, and remind ourselves about what we're all about as Christ-followers.

On *Whac-a-Mole days*, we've got to remember that,

- Jesus teaches us more in the *Whac-a-Mole days* than He does in the *waterslide days*.
- Jesus loves our kids more than we do.
- The whole point of marriage is to teach us about servanthood and sacrifice.
- The hair grows back (*usually*).
- We all get a turn on the small group prayer list.
- We should *whac* at the *mole* and not the *people* around us!

I don't know how deep my relationship with God or my wife would be without *Whac-a-Mole days*. Plus, they make *waterslide days* even more delightful.

Oh-No Admonition

"When he calls out to me, I will answer him; I will be with him in trouble. I will rescue him and give him honor."

(Psalm 91:15)

Oh-No, Aha, and Glory Be

Matt Tullos

A Thanksgiving List

G. K. Chesterton once said, "The worst moment for an atheist is when he is really thankful and has no one to thank."[1] Well, I am not an atheist. I have Someone to thank. But as I've grown older, my gratitude list has become a little unexpected. My gratitude spans over many years, towns, jobs, and circumstances, but only one wife. And I'm thankful for that as well. One wife. I don't know how the "multiple wife" thing would ever really work, and I don't know any Fundamentalist Mormons to ask.

I'm thankful for the unexpected rescues that I've experienced, like the old lady in our church who had the stealth and courtesy to let me know my fly was unzipped before I got up to pray in front of the whole church on Easter Sunday last year. That's called mercy.

And I'm thankful for the fireman who came to our house so quickly after our two-year-old got stuck inside the leg lifter of our recliner several years ago. Don't ask me how he did that. There are certain things toddlers never reveal. I thought they were going to have to come in with the "jaws of life," but it only took a special screwdriver to free the child, and the fireman even stayed to reassemble the chair. That's called grace.

I'm also thankful for my sisters who prepared me for marriage by helping me learn that it's impossible to win an argument with a woman you live with. That's called wisdom.

I'm thankful that most broken electronics are fixed by unplugging them, waiting thirty seconds, and plugging them back in. I'm thankful for the internet and video assembly demonstrations for items that come with French language instruction manuals that only show arrows, slots, and hardware. Otherwise, I'd have a storage room of random, useless parts.

I'm thankful that I didn't win the auditions for several theatre MFA programs after college. I would have never met my wife, and I would probably be doomed to a life of off-off-Broadway productions and bit parts lasting three seconds on CSI as the dead body.

I'm thankful for the near misses, the high school break-ups, the interstate break-downs, freedom from wealth that could have made me over-confident and less hungry, and the times I got sick, which God used as forced Sabbaths when I was too busy. I've come to realize that the blessings of life rarely come from shortcuts, windfalls, and leisure cruises. Instead, I am blessed because of a lot of things that were awkward, uncomfortable, disappointing, and scary. Each moment and person reminds me there was Someone behind the scenes, working all things together for my good. All things—even the unfortunate and slightly embarrassing ones.

Aha Moment

"Rejoice always, pray constantly, give thanks in everything; for this is God's will for you in Christ Jesus."

(1 Thessalonians 5:16-18)

---

[1]. https://www.goodreads.com/quotes/654610-the-worst-moment-for-an-atheist-is-when-he-is

It's All There

Recently we've seen God's Word questioned, defiled, glorified, and deified. It's all caused me to really think through what the Word of God means to me. God's Word is peace to me, but God's Word also disturbs the peace in my life. That's right, it disturbs the peace. It causes me to see the storms. It's constantly stirring me like batter in a bowl—it thickens me.

It tells the whole story. There are lots of things that I would have censored out, but God chose to tell the truth. To record anger so great that it wishes for the death of infants. It shows heroes with flaws. You won't find a Clark Kent type in this book other than Christ, who was the Word. Men and women fail and then succeed. Or they succeed and then fail. It's always a combination of both except for Enoch, and he got a hall pass before the bell rang.

Christians that I'm around today are on a quest for defending the Word of God against heretics. Nothing new to the church. But as Spurgeon once said, *"The Word of God is like a lion. You don't have to defend it, you just have to let it out of the cage."*[2] (How I wish I would have thought of that metaphor! Please forgive the writer envy, sweet Jesus.)

Theologians wield the Word of God as a theological litmus test to keep out people they don't like. We find our favorite parts, parts that fit our general worldview, and we make people sign off on it. Others choose to make the Bible a graven image, worshiping it more than God Himself. Putting their god, the twenty pound version, on the communion table—never read, but ain't it big?

As I read the Acts of the apostles, the major formula of the Holy Spirit is this: the Holy Spirit doesn't have any formulas. Meanwhile, the Acts of the American church is that we are glitzed out, overfed, and underachieving. We are focused on the power of the company (church inc.) rather than the company of His power.

To tell you the truth, the thing I love about God's Word is this: it is unfiltered grace. No deleted scenes. No formulaic ending, no apologies, and no edits. It's the light unto my path. It's a scary book when you get right down to it because it calls for radical love. It propels us to snatch people out of the leper colony and Bethesda's pool of self-help and holistic healing. It leaves the servant work to me. It warns me to avoid debt and riches—both have the potential to damn me. And it dares me to believe in something from nothing, life from death, and beginning from ending.

---

[2] https://www.goodreads.com/quotes/8561226-the-word-of-god-is-like-a-lion-you-don-t

The Bible is anti-religion. It doesn't show God as a tip-toe-through-the-tulips Creator. He's a roaring Lion, and He dares you to battle. Note that His battle is always His. He is not looking for our help. He is inviting us to an adventure so great and unpredictable that even as we gasp our final breath, we look forward to the next page-turning chapter of the swashbuckling thriller. It is not civilized. It is not a book of administration and order. And again I say, it's against religion. (And most will never get their brain around that truth. I pray I will.) The Bible is about dead men walking. It's about surrendering, holding our hands to heaven, and watching our God—like an angry parent witnessing a bully torment his little girl—knock the snot out him and dare him to pull that stunt again. (Therefore, one must examine himself to be sure he is not a bully.)[3]

Some Christians use the Bible as lawyers use precedent to argue their case, citing certain past cases in God's Word as their loophole and syllogism. Usually their case has more to do with their personal power than it has to do with the Great Commission or the greatest commandment. Some of these people would rather see a neighborhood go to hell than have the wrong type of person (sex, race, political faction) preach in the neighborhood. And because of this, they become the practicing liberals in the body.

I must spend more time reading the Word of God than listening to people talk about the Word of God. I must spend more time letting the Word teach me through the Holy Spirit. It's trusting God's promise that the Word will accomplish what it set out to do. And yes, indeed, certainly, and verily I must *do* the Word of God every day.

I look forward to spending more time in God's Word. When I do, it's never wasted time.

Glory Be Declaration

"All Scripture is inspired by God and is profitable for teaching, for rebuking, for correcting, for training in righteousness, so that the man of God may be complete, equipped for every good work."

(2 Timothy 3:16-17)

[3.] We find many bullies in the church these days. Just sayin'.

Forget Resolutions, I'd Like a Time Machine

If there were ever a superpower I've coveted, it would be the ever illusive, never invented time machine. Granted, I wouldn't want to go back to my seventh grade year. I don't think anyone would. And I wouldn't want to stay in the past very long. I enjoy my technology too much to just hang around in the early 2000s with a flip phone and those clunky computer monitors. Going back to last year could offer some amazing possibilities for me, though. I'd even settle on a single email to my last year self. It might go something like this:

> To my last year self,
>
> Contrary to your assumptions, when a rental truck backs into an oak tree, the rental truck is the loser every time. It will crumple like a tin can. And while you're at it, get the rental insurance. It will save you lots of paperwork.
>
> And also, enjoy that subwoofer that you got for your birthday, but skip trying to get your wife to appreciate it as much as you do. She won't. Ever. You shouldn't waste any more time on that one.
>
> And about that "capture the flag" game that you'll play this July with your teenage son and his friends . . . be warned. Behind the neighbor's shrubs you'll be tempted to hurdle, there's a cactus and some gardening tools. It's crazy how one little fact can change everything. And you might want to skip the game altogether. You are a little too old for shenanigans that involve trespassing, flashlights, and emergency room explanations.
>
> Also, when purchasing that romantic Valentine card for Darlene, read the words on the card carefully. Check all pronouns.
>
> And just a few other suggestions, my dear young self (and all other readers):
>
> Stop looking forward to Fridays, and enjoy the whole week. Life's too short to love weekends only.
>
> Protect and value the time you have with your kids. Last year will never happen again, and this year won't either.
>
> Pray as many "Wow, God!" prayers as you do "Help, God!" prayers. There's lots of amazing stuff on the earth to see, so don't just try to survive. Plan to thrive and appreciate the beauty of God's good earth. The art is everywhere.

Aha Moment

"Jesus Christ is the same yesterday, today, and forever."

(Hebrews 13:8)

These are just a few of the things I'd say to my present self. But they all still apply—especially the one about the romantic Valentine cards.

Matt Tullos

Our April Surprise

Easter comes early at our neighborhood discount store. They've been at this Easter thing since February 15th. Since the day after Valentine's, the Easter goods have dominated the center aisles of the store. And believe me, I know the timing. Like most guys, I'm usually there to pick out a couple of last-minute Valentine things, and as I rummage through the cards on aisle fifteen that, by this point, looks as apocalyptic as a teenager's bedroom, I notice through the door of the back room that it's stuffed with Easter baskets, chocolate bunnies, plastic bouquets, egg coloring kits, and pastel candies. All the specialty Peeps are there too. Peeps were once just your basic yellow carbohydrate balls, but now there are blue raspberry Peeps, cotton candy Peeps, fruit punch Peeps, party cake Peeps, sour watermelon Peeps, coconut Peeps, chocolate caramel Peeps, and even "surprise Peeps" . . . and that's just for starters.

As I peek through the little submarine-like window in the back of the pharmacy, I see the Easter inventory staring back at me on carts, packed like sardines. They're just waiting for the clock to strike midnight so they can take over the store. It's so un-Easter like! And I don't just mean that they have missed the whole point of the Resurrection, which they have. But what makes Easter so amazing is that it's so surprising.

The disciples weren't counting down the days until the Resurrection. They didn't gather around the tomb before dawn, waiting for the greatest moment in history. They totally didn't get it. They said that the women who went to the tomb were talking nonsense when they came back after seeing Jesus—*No way! That's crazy talk!* The news seemed just too good to be true. The Resurrection caught the whole universe off guard. Even the guards!

This is the true spirit of the Resurrection morning: dumbfounded surprise! God loves to surprise us. I don't know what surprising thing has happened to you so far this year. It may have been an engagement, an unexpected pregnancy, or a new job. But those are just the little surprises in comparison to what we will celebrate on Easter Sunday. We get to celebrate (once again) that the tomb is empty, and we get God's amazing grace! That surprise lasts forever, and He's got more surprises ahead. And we all get to experience them together—as moms and dads, kids and parents, communities and churches. If you pay attention, you'll begin to notice surprises every single day of the year. But stock up on the yellow Peeps. They're seasonal.

Glory Be Declaration

"For the word of the cross is foolishness to those who are perishing, but it is the power of God to us who are being saved."

(1 Corinthians 1:18)

Yes, I Catastrophize

I've learned a new word this week and realized that it's basically my jam. It's *catastrophizing*. Catastrophizing is when someone assumes that the worst will happen. I'm glad someone created this multisyllabic diagnostic term because now my wife knows what to call the thing that I do so frequently. I don't know how I acquired the skill of creating imagined catastrophe. Oh, but I do it so well.

A few years back, my doctor said if my blood pressure continued to be a problem, he'd have to get me on a pill. I hated the idea of that, and then she suggested that I lose twenty pounds. So (as we catastrophists do) I went overboard and lost thirty in about two months. But there was a problem. I found some kind of growth in the center of my chest. I went back to the doctor, and she diagnosed the issue without even a single scan. "That's not cancer, Matt. That's your sternum."

My most recent catastrophizing began with an email from our executive's administrative assistant: "He'd like to set up two appointments with you next week."

"What's the meeting about?"

"He didn't exactly say," she replied cryptically.

That weekend, waiting was unbearable. I hardly slept a wink. Two mystery meetings with my boss's boss? I had already figured it out. The first would be the "termination meeting," and the second one would be the collection of personal items before being escorted out of the building by Human Resources. I would need to get COBRA insurance. What a terrible acrostic for transitional health insurance! Isn't unemployment scary enough without the word *COBRA*?

I spent the weekend looking through Indeed.com for a job. The only problem is that I found very little that I was qualified to do. *How could I tell my sons? How sad and embarrassing to lay that burden on them! I won't mention it until I have another job. I guess I'll need to sell the house. Yikes! Plus, everybody's going to ask me what happened. And what* did *happen? That's a legitimate question. I thought everything was going great. Did someone spread lies about me? Will I be in the news for something I didn't do? How dare they?! Maybe I should get a blood test before the meeting so that I can prove that I did NOT take the drugs like "who knows" said I did. Will we spend the next few years of my dismal existence in public housing?*

I came to work ready for the worst. The executive had a concerned look on his face: "You OK?"

"Um, I guess. Am I?"

He dismissed the question after staring at me for a second. He wasn't firing me. He wanted me to design a PowerPoint.

"YES! YES! I can create a PowerPoint!" (Cue the orchestral swell of triumphal music.) I glided out of the office as if I had won the lottery. That's just how us catastrophizers roll. But why do I do this? The words of Jesus echoed through my head, *Don't worry about tomorrow.* I had to repent of my catastrophizing. The psalmist writes, "Be still and know that I am God" (Psalm 46:10). My translation: "Just chill. He's got this." He did, and He still does. We all face catastrophes, both small and large, but I am committing that I will deal *only* with the ones that actually happen.

Oh-No Admonition

"Therefore don't worry about tomorrow, because tomorrow will worry about itself. Each day has enough trouble of its own."

(Matthew 6:34)

Oh-no, Aha, and Glory Be

Matt Tullos

Back to School/Worst Day Ever

After a hot summer break, kids are preparing once again to invade the schools with dread, excitement, nervousness, energy, and juice boxes. There's something about mid-August that brings a certain unease. It left its mark on me. Literally. It happened at the start of my first year of junior high school. My dad got a new job in another state, and so the week before school started, we were moving. The great thing about this move was that in the middle of the chaos, I was shuffled off to my grandparents so far into the sticks that I couldn't be contacted to move a single box.

My grandparents lived in a little house in the woods of north Louisiana, complete with a ten-acre pond and a cousin nearby. The day before school was our last day to fish, and so we rose up early. In a crude boat made of a tractor tire and a metal tub (yes, I share the DNA of Larry the Cable Guy), we navigated our way through the dead trees rooted throughout the pond. Then something unexpected happened. We hit a stump filled with yellow jackets. The swarm could rival the plagues of Egypt. My cousin and I both dove out of the boat and into the pond. The result was very visible. The yellow jackets stung what they could: my head. I looked like the Elephant Man with measles. And the next day was the first day at the new school in a new town and at a new address. As fate would have it, I was transported across the state by my grandmother who dropped me off directly at the school where my hideous head would be the talk of everyone in the seventh grade. In fact, I still have a few tiny scars on my forehead today.

After school, I rode the bus home, but I had forgotten my new address. So, as I remember it, I just took a stab at where to get off and spent the next hour trying to muster the courage to knock on a stranger's door and ask to phone home. Looking like E.T., it seemed to be the right course of action. It was the worst day of my life up to that point. But one good thing came from it. Years later I'd have a story to share when my kids experienced humiliation. I not only could say, "Wow, that's got to be tough," but I could say, "I know how you feel." First day of middle school is bad. Looking like a Halloween mask on the first day of school? Well, there had to be some use for that day.

I think that's really the beauty of the gospel. When I'm in a really dark place, Jesus doesn't just sympathize and say, *Wow, that's got to be tough.* I can sense Him pointing to the cross that's hanging on the kitchen wall and saying, *I know how you feel.* And that, my brothers and sisters, is good news.

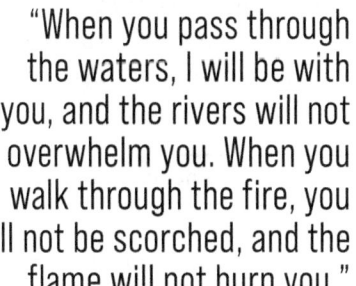

Aha Moment

"When you pass through the waters, I will be with you, and the rivers will not overwhelm you. When you walk through the fire, you will not be scorched, and the flame will not burn you."

(Isaiah 43:2)

Elbow Room and Warp Speed

In bed, the alarm rings, and I feel as if my body is one hundred eighty pounds of cement. God whispers, *What did you expect? You haven't taken a day off in twelve days.*

Ouch!

That morning, I asked,

> *Do I have to run quickly to and fro?*
> *Do I have to get up today and go?*
> *I'd rather throw bed sheets over my head*
> *Or visit the zoo with my boys instead.*
> *I'd hand my to-dos to a wart-covered toad*
> *And chat with a neighbor just down the road.*
> *I'd rather run in the fields of my youth.*
> *I'd rather be 20, to tell you the truth.*
> *I'd rather sneak off with a tall stack of books*
> *And give the librarian puzzling looks.*
> *I'd rather discuss life with a glass of iced tea*
> *With someone as incredibly burned out as me.*
> *I'd rather hike the Grand Canyon today*
> *But I don't have gas money so I guess that I'll stay.*

Life, in an average twenty-first-century family, blows out of our window at one hundred fifty miles an hour. We barely give ourselves the elbow room to really succeed. I know that this is a major character flaw of many guys. As men, husbands, dads, and employees, we instinctively find our self-worth in doing more than just being. We rush! We often forget that being overwhelmed is not Christlikeness.[4] Sometimes I wonder how many opportunities I missed because of the words *have to*, *ought to*, and *gotta*. God meant

---

[4] This is not in the Bible! "Thus Jesus hurriedly got up, realizing what an important day this was going to be. He ran to Galilee, and there He created thirteen lesson parchments, visited fifteen lepers, and had a confrontation therefore with Judas who wasn't behaving and in whom he feared greatly. Hitherto, Jesus went in haste to the zealots committee where He talked for three hours. He encountered many voice messages from the throngs of Judeans and tried to return all of them with at least a beatitude or a warning. Exhausted, the disciples verily tried to keep up with the Son of God, but nay, they could not. They marveled at His time management skills and His strength in persuasive skills. People flocked to Him and stayed with Him, for they knew that if He could accomplish such management tasks with great haste, effort, and fluidity, He knew the habits for being an effective person."

for you to leave room for Him to work. If we don't, our prayer life, our parenting, our marriage, and our future all suffer.

Our best days are marked in moments that usually don't happen because we had more important things to do. We look at our kids, in every life stage, and wonder if they'll ever grow up, and then, before we know it, we realize . . . they did.

Every man I know seems to think he has a warp-speed button. Perhaps that's why we love the idea of superpowers and action heroes. I must confess, I press the warp-speed button far too often. But the reverse gear is nonexistent. We don't get any do-overs for yesterday.

So from today on, I promise to look at all the incredible blessings that are buried under my to-do lists and agendas and behind the billboards that blur across the windshield as I shift into fifth on the open road.

I will try to give more than I get. I can't keep it anyway. God is planning a huge end-of-the-earth bonfire. Even the scented candles and rare works of art my wife bought for next to nothing on eBay will be ashes. I will make it job number one to hang on for dear life to my family, my friends, my mission, and my Jesus. Everything else I'll move to the back of the line.

Glory Be Declaration

"Teach us to number our days carefully so that we may develop wisdom in our hearts."

(Psalm 90:12)

Pray Something!

Martin Luther said, "To be a Christian without prayer is no more possible than to be alive without breathing." I believe it, but I also have to confess that I've gone through long periods of time holding my breath. I'm committed to pray more. I have no excuse because I've been at it for a long time. I started praying when the bell bottoms and Bee Gees were all the rage. Here are a few misconceptions that still trip me up every now and then:

Sometimes I'm a little intimidated talking to God about the latest pride-swallowing struggle in the office when I know this same God might have bigger fish to fry, like the White House, nuclear warheads, and murder hornets. I tend to forget how great the omniscience and sovereignty of God really is. Does He *really* want to hear about my psoriasis flare-ups? Yes. You don't. But He does.

I often place a premium on public prayers. But scripture makes it clear that private praying is where the action is. You've heard those public prayers that really aren't even prayers. I have to smile when I hear those announcement prayers at church. *Lord, we pray that You will bless this offering we give to You. And help our men as they gather for the men's breakfast at 7 a.m. this Friday, with a cost of six dollars per person, and guests eat free.* Wow. I see what you did there. Sometimes our prayers are unintentionally hilarious. *Lord, forgive us of the things we don't do. And help us with the things we* do *do.* It just sounds wrong, doesn't it?

I'm convinced that most of our prayers are confined to prayer emojis on our social media feeds with promises to pray, and yet by the time our head hits the pillow, we don't realize our mindfulness to pray for that need we saw flew out the window on the drive back home. I have a buddy who no longer says, "I'll pray about that." He just starts praying the second after he hears a need. I saw him at the diner one afternoon, and I asked him to pray for my sister who, at the time, had Covid. He took his cap off, stood up, and was off to the races, interceding loudly in front of the breadsticks and everybody. It was awesome. He just grew tired of making prayer promises.

So for now, I've set up a reminder alarm on my phone, and I'm determined to kick it up a notch. No more worrying about public praying and obsessing over every little word that I say. No more promising to pray because I'm *way* too forgetful. I'm setting an empty chair in front of me and closing my door, and I'll just talk to Him like He is my father. And, of course, He is.

Glory Be Declaration

"Pray at all times in the Spirit with every prayer and request, and stay alert with all perseverance and intercession for all the saints."

(Ephesians 6:18)

Matt Tullos

More on Frank

I've never understood the dog. I didn't really like him as much as others in this house, but over a period of months, I became the object of worship. He picked me out and said, *He's mine!* This weenie dog couldn't wait for me to sit down. He hated it when I sat in a desk chair. He was more at peace when I sat on the couch so he could rest his head on my lap. He freaked when I left in the morning, and he celebrated my arrival in the evening. He was the most emotionally needy, dependent creature I've ever met. He wouldn't be ignored.

There were days when I failed. He just overlooked those things and accepted me as I am. He couldn't care less if I got a raise. He had no idea how many followers I had in the Twitter sphere. As far as he was concerned, he was the only one who followed me. *Everywhere.*

My family is a lot smarter than the dog was, but they too offer almost as much grace as Frank our dachshund. Kids are much more interested in my time than my accomplishments.

Frank has gone to whatever place dogs go. (It's not a theological question I spend a lot of time on.) But he marked his territory, most requiring deodorizers.

My kids have left their mark as well. There are holes in the wall from capture the flag during an extended power outage. There are knicks in the coffee table from late night history projects. There are trees that are recovering from the weight of *Tarzan* movie projects. I'll catch up on all the repairs. Someday. Maybe. But we all miss the memories of Frank, the Dad-worshiping canine. The one whose life was a mess during the days I was out of town. I think he somehow got what life was all about—chasing squirrels and fighting dogs four times his size.

Lord, I pray this insane prayer. Make me like him. Keep me so focused on Your presence that I can't stand being away from You. Lord, I focus my eyes on You, waiting, wagging, and wondering when I'll see Your face.

Oh-No Admonition

"He said, 'If you will carefully obey the Lord your God, do what is right in his sight, pay attention to his commands, and keep all his statutes, I will not inflict any illnesses on you that I inflicted on the Egyptians. For I am the Lord who heals you.'"

(Exodus 15:26)

Oh-No, Aha, and Glory Be

Matt Tullos

Read Me First

We recently moved out of state for a new job. It's difficult for me to move away from a familiar place because I always have a lot of explaining to do. I should come with a *Read Me First* list stapled to my shirt when I arrive to work. I think it would probably read something like,

This guy gets lost and loses things. A LOT. He is a hard worker but a little scatterbrained. He is an excellent righter but he mispells. (See what I did there?) He's a speaker, but he's often painfully introverted. He's always had a difficult time saying "no," which sometimes causes him to be overwhelmed. And he has a hard time with zippers.

Yes, zippers would be on the *Read Me First* list. I heard someone ask a famous pastor a deep, spiritual question in a roundtable event: "What's the first thing you do before you get up to speak?" He pondered for a moment and said, "I check my fly." I think that's excellent advice and something I do every time I stand up to make a presentation.

It's comforting to know that God uses deeply flawed people. No one knows how deeply flawed we are better than our spouses and children. I think that's one of the great things about family. They keep us grounded when we get a little too impressed with ourselves. They've seen me back a church bus into a motel. Yes . . . a motel. My wife has had to pick me up at the hospital after a deacon visit because I couldn't remember where I parked my car. Losing a key is interesting. Losing a car? That's a work of art.

Yes, my family has lots of stories on me, but one thing I try to avoid is being a cautionary tale. Cautionary tales are important, but who wants to be one? In the middle of one of Jesus's messages, there is a short, three-word verse. It registers as the second shortest verse in the Bible: Luke 17:32. It says, "Remember Lot's wife." If you are big on memorizing a verse a week, there's an easy verse.

Every time I think of doing something really stupid, I think about that verse. I'd love to purchase it as framed office décor, but it's not sold on Amazon. Why would I want to hang that verse in front of my desk next to pictures of my boys? Simple. I would deplore the fact that people would use my downfall as a sordid illustration of what good men are capable of doing. "Remember Darlene's husband." That would be mortifying. It's a powerful verse that has saved my scalp when I've circled the wagons during a time of temptation. You can always go to the hardware store to buy extra keys, but my wife, my kids, and my heritage? They are irreplaceable.

Oh-No Admonition

"So, whoever thinks he stands must be careful not to fall."

(1 Corinthians 10:12)

The Returns Department: A Christmas Dream

It's not often that you find yourself walking through the mall with an archangel. But that's the way dreams are, aren't they? Everything seems real, and then your dream throws in something odd—like going to school in only your underwear or discovering that your teeth are falling out. In the dream, the angel winked at me and said, "Well, looks like you survived another last-minute shopping spree."

"I never was much of a planner," I replied.

"You've got way too much stuff," Gabriel said, pointing to a shopping cart filled with beautifully wrapped boxes.

"Those aren't mine."

"Yes they are."

"But—"

"Don't argue with an archangel," Gabriel said with a chuckle. "Seriously, they are yours, and you might want to return them."

We arrived in front of the smallest shop tucked next to a department store. The sign simply said, RETURNS. The man greeted Gabriel with a smile and said, "We meet again."

Gabriel got straight to the point. "This fellow has a number of things he'd like to return."

"What are you talking about? I've never seen these boxes in my life!" I exclaimed as I surveyed the beautifully decorated presents. It was then that I noticed the tag on the box wrapped in reindeer paper: ENVY.

Gabriel sighed and said, "You've had that one hanging around as long as I've known you. You've concealed it with a veneer of kudos, applause, and congratulations, but deep inside you feel rotten. It turns everything into a competition, and you always feel like the loser."

The returns assistant smiled and said, "So you are returning ENVY."

"He is."

"And the reason for the return?"

"It doesn't fit him."

Gabriel paused for a moment and then pulled out an ornately wrapped box with the tag: SHAME.

"This has a lot of moving parts. Most of them are under the surface of the item," Gabriel explained. "He's had it since childhood, and now he needs to let it go back where it came from."

"And the reason for the return?" the assistant asked as he scribbled down notes.

"It doesn't work."

"He's right," I added.

For a long time, as dreams go, we emptied the seemingly bottomless cart of packages and provided reasons for the record: BITTERNESS ("it's so very old school"), ACCLAIM ("it doesn't do what they said it would do on TV"), FEAR ("too many side effects when he uses it"), ANGER ("it's just ugly; who would want that . . . really"), and a flood of smaller items that are too many to name. After the cart was empty, a feeling of lightness enveloped me. I was beginning to experience what Christmas was all about. As I surveyed the brightly decorated packages, the assistant of the Returns Shop said, "I wish we could reimburse you for these, but they aren't worth a plug nickel."

As we walked away, I asked a million questions, and Gabriel answered them all. He revealed mysteries great and small. Answers to a thousand questions. But for the life of me, I can't remember any of them. Isn't that just the way dreams are?

Oh-No Admonition

"Therefore, since we also have such a large cloud of witnesses surrounding us, let us lay aside every hindrance and the sin that so easily ensnares us. Let us run with endurance the race that lies before us."

(Hebrews 12:1)

Oh-No, Aha, and Glory Be

The Blessing of Stuck

It's not often that I get to rescue my wife. She's not your prototypical damsel in distress. But today I got my opportunity. She was late for a meeting and ran out of gas on the side of a busy country road. I got in my Forerunner and ran. It was really kind of exciting. The "Find a Friend" app on my smartphone gave me her exact location, and once I got there, I pulled off the road and filled her tank with enough gas to get her on her way. She left immediately to her meeting after smothering me with compliments, apologies, and kisses. I got back into my vehicle, and, wouldn't you know it, I was stuck in the mud. The next thing I knew, *I* was the damsel in distress. I did all the things I thought to do. Forward, reverse, rocking back and forth between the two gears. I even put the Forerunner in neutral and tried to push it out of the mud. This was the height of hubris and the depth of self-awareness. I'm not a man of steel, but for a fleeting moment, I thought I was.

Finally, a kind citizen came by in his truck to see if he could help me. I must have looked pitiful with mud splashes up to my kneecaps. He pulled over to the side of the road, got a chain hooked around my SUV, and put it into drive. But, alas, the same thing happened to him. He was six inches deep in mud. His four-wheel drive couldn't drive either. Then a smaller vehicle pulled over, perhaps curious to see what had happened, and he got stuck. And so, then there were three. We spent the next fifteen minutes convincing passersby not to stop and get stuck like we did. It wasn't an easy task because mudding is a year-round pastime in these parts. We were three strangers who sadly and unwittingly entered the Tennessee version of the Bermuda Triangle. We were at the mercy of a higher power: a tow truck.

This entire experience was a simple metaphor of life in all its complexities, chaos, and wonder. It brought along its own moral: *Sometimes when you try to help people, you get stuck yourself.* I've had this experience before. I've tried to help somebody get unstuck only to discover my own pitifully enormous capacity to get stuck. I had good intentions but lacked the self-awareness. *Let he who drives take heed lest he get stuck.* That's my new version of 1 Corinthians 10:12. The experience also reminded me about everything that's great about church and family. We're ordinary people with a natural inclination to get stuck and go it alone. When we confess our "stuckness" and our powerlessness, He has the towing capacity to lift us from the mirey clay every time.

Glory Be Declaration

"He brought me up from a desolate pit, out of the muddy clay, and set my feet on a rock, making my steps secure."

(Psalm 40:2)

PART 2:
Marriage

Oh-No: We are so different!
Aha: Maybe that was the whole point.
Glory Be: God was the matchmaker.

Sure, we've had our moments where it would have seemed to make more sense to throw in the towel, but what a gigantic mistake it would have been! The payoff is overwhelming; the memories are indelible. When you hear the songs, live the stories, do your dance, and share life together, year after year, decade after decade, those moments will only mean that much more.

Those Looks

Do you remember the first time she looked at you and you looked at her? Perhaps your story goes something like this:

At first there was the glance. I saw her in a crowded room. Through the noise and the obstacles, I saw her. I was suspended in time—weightless. It was back when we both were skinny—motionless. I was frozen by her beauty, or maybe the air-conditioning was up too high.

There I was. And there she was. We were both there, together, and yet we knew not each other. We were void of relationship status and even friend requests. We were strangers.

I glanced. She glanced. Oh, what glances!

At first, short glances, but very soon the glances turned into stares. We stared at each other, and we liked what we saw. We stared over dinner at fancy restaurants. We stared at each other during church when we should have been staring at the pastor. I would even stare during football games. She would even stare during clearance sales.

We ogled. Funny word, but quite fitting: *ogle*. Webster defines it as, "to stare with great desire." We were in love! Then we wanted to see more of each other. We desired each other. We wanted to stare at each other all the time—day and night, in sickness and in health, till death do us part. So we stared at the altar, and we received a license to stare. Then, shortly after we received permission to stare—day and night, night and day, aaaaaaall the time—we saw everything!

Then, *Oh-No:* The stares turned into glares.

> He: "Sorry I'm late! We played an extra nine holes."
> She: Glare!
> He: "Happy birthday, honey. You'll love this new power drill I bought you!"
> She: Glare!
> He: "How about tonight?"
> She: "I'm too tired."
> He: Glare.

She remembers the times when he once glanced her way and said, "Wow!"

He remembers the time she used to love to look at him, and now it seems that the only time she looks is when she wants something.

She says, "Not only do you not look at me, you don't even look at what I do! You think clean socks just fly from the hamper into the washer, then to the dryer, and then back to the magic drawer."

He says, "She looked at me with such respect! Now she doesn't even care about my needs."

She says, "Making love . . . what a misnomer! It's turned into a duty. How can I enjoy intimacy with someone who doesn't even look at me—deeply?"

He says, "Before I was married, I used to laugh at the way the King James Version describes sex as knowing. Now I understand. How can you make love with someone who doesn't even know you . . . much less someone who doesn't look at you? Is there a cure for blindness? Is there a surgery that can remove emotional cataracts?"

In marriage, we forget that it all started with a glance. Can we find that glance? Will we look at each other? Deeply? Will we?

The *Aha* of any marriage is that we can find that look of love again.

That look—the fire of the relationship lost because of circumstances, hurt, fear, anger, and misunderstandings. That look can be found through Christ.

Aha Moment

"Therefore, if anyone is in Christ, he is a new creation; the old has passed away, and see, the new has come! Everything is from God, who has reconciled us to himself through Christ and has given us the ministry of reconciliation."

(2 Corinthians 5:17-18)

Oh-No, Aha, and Glory Be

Matt Tullos

It's Gotta Be the Shoes

My wife has the spiritual gift of accessorizing. It's more than jewelry; it's also shoes. I'm a basic *three pair of shoes* dude. I never even noticed that Darlene had so many shoes when we were engaged. Maybe I was subliminally attracted to her because of the shoes. I don't know. But wow. We moved last year, and there were about as many shoe boxes as there were boxes in the warehouse of the last scene of *The Raiders of the Lost Ark*. Leather boots, high heels, dress-up sneakers, clogs, crocs, ballerina flats, earth shoes, flip-flops, galoshes, moccasins, slippers, oxfords, saddle shoes, derbies, ankle boots, platforms, loafers, and lots of different colors for every ensemble you could imagine.

She slowly evolved me into having more shoes. I have six pairs of shoes now. I had no idea that your shoes had to match your belt. All those years of doing it wrong.... But ten pairs. That's where I draw the line. I don't like making decisions in the morning. I figure I can only make about ten decisions a day, and I don't want to waste all my decisions on footwear.

When she was pregnant, Darlene had another line of shoes that was a different size and style to be more accommodating to swelling and discomfort. She still has those pregnancy-era shoes which, I must confess, makes me a little nervous. It's true, she has a hard time letting go of shoes.

The other day I walked into her closet, which is about the size of our first apartment. (That says more about our first apartment than her closet.) I got a little emotional as I looked at all those shoes. I thought about all the places I've followed those little feet of hers. We've been on mission trips, to youth camp, on vacations, to ball games, to rodeos, on nature trails, to grocery runs, and to worship services. They reminded me of the times that she kicked my leg under the table before I said a little too much at a dinner party. She's kind of like the Holy Ghost that way. I thought about the times she'd take off her shoes on occasions when we felt like we were on holy ground. I didn't wonder what I would do with all that space if her shoes weren't there. Rather, I thought about what I would do if the owner of the shoes wasn't there. It made me want to take her to the outlet store and get another six or seven pairs. I don't want to walk a mile in her shoes. That would be painful and embarrassing. But I do want to walk with her as many miles as I can.

Aha Moment

"Then the Lord God said, 'It is not good for the man to be alone. I will make a helper corresponding to him.'"

(Genesis 2:18)

I Can Say Never

In marriage, there's a rule you must follow. Eliminate the words *always* and *never*. In other words, don't say to your wife, "You're never ready when I'm ready to leave." That's a buzzkill right off the bat. Plus, it's just not true. *Never* is a very difficult word when it comes to speaking truth. I used to say that the Cubs would never win a World Series, and history had my back. The Cubs hadn't won a World Series since 1908. It hadn't happened in over a hundred years! But 2016 changed all that. The curse ended, and the Cubs were champs. There's a chance that in your marriage, the universe shifted, and your wife waited on you. *Never* doesn't work. It's insulting, and it's just fake news. But there are times when you should adhere to *nevers*. These are the good *nevers* of marriage:

Never re-preach a message to your spouse on Sunday.

Example: The wife says to the husband, "That was a powerful message on idolatry. Don't you think your fixation on your bass boat kind of . . . well . . . ." Stop right there. He's got the Holy Spirit to convict him, and a wife being a human highlighter pen is not helping.

Never telegraph your anger in cryptic, coded actions.

Guys, when your wife offends thee, avoid walking around doing huffy things like shutting closet doors a little more strongly than usual, answering innocent questions sarcastically, or in worse cases, throwing the garbage can lids on the roof of your house. Leave the word *huffy* with the bicycles. After decades of practice, I've found a much better communication method: USE WORDS.

Never assume he's heard you the first time.

Most men have an ability to go into completely different universes when performing even the most menial tasks. Most women can text, talk on the phone, change a diaper, and fix a broken piece of china with superglue all at the same time. For most men, it's like this: "Everybody be quiet and give me room. I'm organizing my socks!" Most of us can't even comprehend the cerebral gymnastics of multitasking. If he's doing anything, even clipping his toenails, ask him to stop, then grab his face with the palms of your hands, and speak slowly.

There are plenty of *nevers* in marriage, just not the kind of *nevers* you say in arguments. There are also some incredible *always* rules that can make your marriage sizzle. Always encourage. Always forgive. Always put the toilet seat down. Always seek to improve your connection. Always work together in parenting. And always love. And the greatest of these is *always* love.

Glory Be Declaration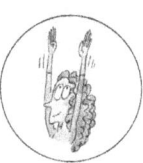

"In the same way, husbands are to love their wives as their own bodies. He who loves his wife loves himself. For no one ever hates his own flesh but provides and cares for it, just as Christ does for the church, since we are members of his body. For this reason a man will leave his father and mother and be joined to his wife, and the two will become one flesh. This mystery is profound, but I am talking about Christ and the church. To sum up, each one of you is to love his wife as himself, and the wife is to respect her husband."

(Ephesians 5:28-33)

Oh-No, Aha, and Glory Be

Sometimes It Takes a Tornado

March of 2020 was crazy in my neck of the woods. Come to think of it, it was crazy in everybody's neck of the woods to be honest.[5] Right? But before all the sheltering in place, toilet paper panics, and cancelations of modern life, we had a weather event. A tornado ripped a path through our town. We were blessed that we didn't have any major damage. Dave, a friend of mine, faired a lot worse. After the storm, a farmer who lived around thirty miles away mailed him back some bank statements and tax documents that he found in his field. I'm not joking. It happened. This was a full-on *Wizard of Oz*, granny-in-a-rocking-chair-outside-the-window kind of tornado.

But for us, it was just a loss of power. One moment we were watching the reports on the TV, scanning our friends' Facebook posts, streaming music, microwaving leftovers, and doing some picture hanging with the power drill, and the next minute we were both huddled around the flashlight on my phone that was quickly losing battery life. Everything stopped, and it stayed that way for twelve hours. We were prepared for these moments in Louisiana with a generator, but in Tennessee, we totally didn't expect it. We sold our generator when we left.

So there we were . . . no TV, internet, lights, or hot food. We were now living like my great-grandparents. Twenty-first-century "life" just came to a screeching halt. We cuddled in our empty nest in the dark at 1 a.m., thrust into the stone age without flint to spark a fire. Then we started to do something. We started talking to each other. I mean *really* talking. No alerts from our phones, no music, no interruptions, no other activities. For the first thirty minutes it was mortifying. I just wasn't used to it. Where was all the ambient noise? Would we survive without hot showers, hair dryers, and Hot Pockets™? Amazingly we managed to see another tomorrow. In fact, we rediscovered each other in the night. We talked about all the things we had experienced over the decades of pee-wee sports, carpools, health scares, and relocations. In other words, all those things a large family goes through in a year and sometimes in a month. We prayed for each other and for those who would have it a lot worse than we did when the sun came back up. In truth, it was one of our best nights as a couple because we actually stopped multitasking and discovered each other again.

Sometimes it takes a tornado to get us to really listen and enjoy each other. We plan our power outages now on a routine basis without the assistance of tornadoes. We shut everything down so that we can enjoy God and each other. And that's kind of the whole point of marriage, isn't it?

Oh-No Admonition

"Finally, all of you be like-minded and sympathetic, love one another, and be compassionate and humble."

(1 Peter 3:8)

[5.] If for some reason you can't remember 2020, Google *Covid-brain*. Still don't remember? You might have been on a desert island with a volleyball named Wilson.

Matt Tullos

She Asked Me a Question

I have a particular skill. A skill I have acquired over a long marriage" (said in my best Liam Neeson voice). It's a detrimental skill:

I have the fascinating gift of looking like I'm listening with all the non-verbal signals of head nodding, eye-contact, and vocal cues like "hmm," "oh," and "really," while actually not listening.

My wife could be sharing her concerns about the policies of our health care plan, or the excess suds produced by the new dishwashing detergent, while inside my brain I am wondering if the Saints will ever win another Superbowl. I especially regret this particular skill when I hear Darlene's voice trail up in the form of a question. I don't have any idea what she asked or even what she was talking about because I wasn't listening. This happened a lot. At least once a week.

This has been a source of irritation for my wife. I have suggested several solutions, such as emailing me bullet points, creating PowerPoints for couples dialogue, using sports metaphors in conversations, and squeezing my arm tightly when I really, *really* need to know something she's saying. Curiously, she didn't take to any of those ideas.

Instead, she signed us up to go to a listening conference. I was a little perplexed. Isn't that what you do when you go to any conference? You listen. But no. This is a conference where the topic is *how* to listen. It was a great experience, but I have never reached the level of exhaustion that I did this past weekend at the conference. I listened more over the weekend than I usually do over the span of a year. We mirrored. That's when you repeat what your spouse said and then ask, "Did I get that?" Then, if I didn't get it, Darlene would repeat what she said. Then, after I got it, I'd ask, "Is there more?" Which is a necessary and yet dumb question. There's *always* more. And then I would mirror the rest of the stuff.

I am slowly learning how to listen actively and with empathy. It was an amazing weekend, to be honest. I learned so much more about my wife, and I'm learning the more I listen, the more intimacy we feel as a couple. And so naturally the more I meet her needs, the more my needs are met in the marriage. Which is . . . well . . . you know . . . .

I'm taming my one-track, ADHD, distracted, disorganized, cluttered mind, and I'm finding that there is a lot more room up there when I settle down and simply listen. You might even say that I have a particular set of listening skills. Skills that I acquired over a very long weekend.

I must go for now. Darlene is in the other room, and I think she just asked me a question. I have no idea what it was about.

Oh-No Admonition

"My dear brothers and sisters, understand this: Everyone should be quick to listen, slow to speak, and slow to anger, for human anger does not accomplish God's righteousness."

(James 1:19-20)

I'm a Turtle! She's a Tiger!

I heard at a marriage conference that two people often marry: one who is like a turtle and one who is like a tiger. In adversity, the tiger goes into attack mode under stress. The claws come out, and it gets loud. The turtle, however, in times of stress, crawls into the safety of the hard shell of avoidance, refuses to confront, and eats a lot of cheese.

I confess that I am a turtle, and Darlene, well . . . she's a tiger. She wants to engage, and I want to run to the storm shelter when dark clouds appear in the western sky.

I can think of no better example of this than my weekend in Indianapolis. We had just finished a crosstown move. I hate moving. Yes, *hate*. I don't like the boxes, the rented implements, the trucks, the smell, the back strain, and the shameless begging for friends to help. It was a tough move. My wife is the move administrator, and, of course, I am the muscles of the operation. We ended our day of moving after five truckloads. Oh, the joy of completion! At 1 a.m. I returned the rental truck and collapsed on a bare mattress under a thick blue industrial moving blanket. All our worldly possessions surrounded us in a varied collection of boxes.

The next morning, I was to leave to speak at a pastors' conference in Indy. This was something we knew months before. Darlene wasn't happy about it but understood that it was planned long before our one-day moving extravaganza.

Once I got to Indianapolis, I received a call from the rental company. The gruff voice on the other end asked, "When are you going to return the truck?"

I could have just died! *The truck? I turned it in last night.*

"We don't see it here."

"Check the lot," I said.

Let me explain that this is the biggest truck rental outlet in the known world. I'm sure of it. From the main office to the outer regions of the gargantuan lot, nothing could be seen but orange trucks of all sizes.

It gets worse. Day two of the conference, after I had left twenty-three messages pleading for an update, I received a voicemail from the Nashville police saying that they had a warrant for my arrest for the theft of "said sixteen foot truck!"

The blood rushed from my face, and I saw my career pass before me with the clarity of a near death experience. I was in full freak-out mode and went into the turtle shell of doom.

Little did the truck company or Nashville's finest know that I married a tiger. While I was having a bag-over-the-head, Barney Fife panic attack, my wife went to work. While I wanted to run to the backside of the desert, what does Mrs. Tiger do? She went straight to the news desk of the local ABC affiliate. I have no idea how the conversation went down after the well-known lead anchor called the moving company and said, "I understand that you have an arrest warrant out on a local pastor," but within ten minutes, they found the truck in one of their garages getting serviced.

The police detective called me soon after, even before my wife did. "Well, looks like they misplaced your truck on their lot and found it. This is the first time I've heard of a company doing that to a preacher, and I've had lots of weird accusations in my career." The nervous general manager gushed with apologies. "You can have a free rental any time you want." I laughed inside and thought, *Wow, they met my wife!*

I literally fell to my knees in the hotel room. I said, "Lord, you know I've complained to You about this tiger I married, but today I realized I married way above my pay grade. I repent!"

Sometimes it takes very diverse personalities to make a marriage. Mine's one. You see, if she wasn't a tiger, I could still be paying on a truck I rented for one day from a shady rental truck corporation after I got out of the truck theft halfway house in East Nashville.

Glory Be Declaration

"A man who finds a wife finds a good thing and obtains favor from the LORD."
(Proverbs 18:22)

I Get His Point

My wife and I have always had an ongoing feud. It has consumed our time. It springs up almost monthly. We have talked about it incessantly for twenty-eight years now. I have emailed her my point of view, and still, there it is. Staring us right in the face. Issue: the validity of the musical as a legitimate art form. I know. I have a losing case. Musicals are everywhere. I just don't have a great appreciation for them. I just can't get my brain around someone during an intense moment of great consequence or extreme emotion bursting out in song. I find it hard to make sense out of that one.

OK, OK, I know. That's a lame issue to spend any amount of time or energy on. Seriously though, I have often tripped over my desire to make a point, some of lesser importance than the worth of musical theater! Whether it's about schedules, priorities, or the safest way to merge, *if only my wife would get it*. If she could see the point I'm trying to make in this little debate we're having, things would be soooo much better. My point is logical. My point is practical. I have several sub-points and side-points. I have crunched the numbers, measured the meaning, and scratched the surface. My argument is logical, practical, yes, even spiritual. I am methodical with my point-making. I state my case, I stand my ground, and I land my thesis. 'Nuf said. Right?

What I often fail to realize is that marriage was never intended to be a contest, a debate, or a hierarchy. It is and has always been about a sacrificial metaphor of God's love. But I have to confess I often forget that when we are deciding how we are going to spend our time, money, or energy. I confess that it's often easy to forget sacrificial love when the game is on or the checking account is low or the agenda for the day is completely about everyone else. So difficult! And I feel so yucky the morning after, during my quiet time. And then I get to do that other hard thing—plan a time to repent and reconcile. I don't even like to think about that at 6 a.m. It's not fun, and every now and then it's not even fair. One thing's for certain: you can never, *ever* win a marital argument. Winning doesn't promote love and intimacy. In other words, guys, "right" ain't sexy.

God uses marriage to show me how selfish I can be, even when I'm right. And then God reminds me about what really makes Him pleased in me. He's pleased when He sees that I am following His lead. The amazing thing about the whole context of marriage is that when I follow the lead of Christ in my life, my wife will begin to follow my lead as a husband. That's how it's set up, and the more I remember this, the easier it is to stop making a point and start making a marriage.

Oh-No Admonition

"Let all bitterness, anger and wrath, shouting and slander be removed from you, along with all malice."

(Ephesians 4:31)

Matt Tullos

It's the Big One

It's Valentine's again, and my wife deserves the very best, but it is absolutely amazing how February 14th approaches with the velocity of gazelles. *I just conquered Christmas shopping! Couldn't we celebrate Valentine's in October as kind of a warmup Christmas when our list has more names on it?* Christmas is a team sport with lots or people, blitzes, screens, and sacks. Valentine's is a high-stakes solo sport.

It's always fun to hang out at the Walgreens® on February 13th to see the legion of men skulking in the card section, trying not to look embarrassed. There's a man code in there. *Look only at the cards, not the other men.* Kind of like a Baptist at a liquor store. *Act normal. No talking! We're all reading here.* This is serious business, not an opportunity to get to know each other or share tips. Yes, for men, Valentine's Day is a solo sport. You are out there alone, pal, with your creativity, memory, swagger, and debit card. It can't look mechanical. And for goodness sakes, no gift cards! Gift cards say, *I love you, but I also don't want to think.* It's got to feel organic—and not organic as in, the roses must be hormone free. Your gestures must be planned well in advance and from your heart, not Lionel Richie's.

Also, personalize the card. Don't just sign your name. And say something romantic that's not from the Song of Solomon. Most things in that book don't translate. Don't tell your wife that her hair is like a flock of goats (6:5). Don't tell her that her navel is like a goblet or that her waist is like a mound of wheat (7:2). Don't tell her that her nose is like a tower of Lebanon (7:4). None of these verses are helpful.

Instead, live out 1 Corinthians 13 every day of the year. If you do that, Valentine's Day is a cinch. Just read the cards very carefully, and write something amazing in your own chicken scratch. Shower her with love and flowers. And who knows? You might just get lucky.

Aha Moment

"Then he said to them, 'Go and eat what is rich, drink what is sweet, and send portions to those who have nothing prepared, since today is holy to our Lord. Do not grieve, because the joy of the Lord is your strength.'"
(Nehemiah 8:10)

Oh-No, Aha, and Glory Be

BlissCoin

A couple of years ago, I had some equipment for sale, and this guy messaged me and asked if I would want to sell it for some Bitcoin. He started explaining it. The words he used were English, but my brain could no more process the sentences than it could process Mandarin Chinese. Back then, I hadn't even heard of Bitcoin, and the more I investigated it, the more confused I got! It was defined as a type of digital currency in which a record of transactions is maintained, and new units of currency are generated by the computational solution of mathematical problems, and which operates independently of a central bank.[6]

It sounds like a cross between Monopoly money and my ninth grade algebra that I had to take twice. A totally bogus proposition if you ask me. And the other part about being operated outside of a central bank is it sounds like you are working for a part of the mob, or you are buying groceries with 1990s Pokémon cards. I was totally not interested.

But there is a currency that's outside a central bank that married couples use all the time: *BlissCoin*. BlissCoins are those investments we make in our spouse that lead to the marital bliss we seek. You may not know about BlissCoin, but if you're married you already use it. It's worth a lot, and it's pretty easy to invest.

- Remembering and planning way ahead for special dates will get you about 10 BlissCoins. Pretty Sweet!
- Cleaning up your six-year-old's vomit on the hardwood floor: 30–3,000 BlissCoins, depending on how squeamish your spouse is.
- Guys, for your wife, really listening to her without looking at your phone is an easy 5 BlissCoins.
- Listening without getting defensive as she shares a hurt you caused can gain you 20 BlissCoins. Be careful here; if you can't do this, it might just land you in the BlissCoin doghouse, and the accommodations are awful!
- Saying I love you first, 2 BlissCoins.
- Showing you love him or her, at least 8 BlissCoins.
- Praying with your spouse? Well, it's hard to calculate, but it's in the thousands.

This matrimonial exchange system varies from couple to couple, but it's always wise to invest in BlissCoin. When you invest in your marriage, the interest accrues throughout your life. Besides, you might do something really dumb, and having the BlissCoin is a handy thing to have around.

Aha Moment

"One person gives freely, yet gains more; another withholds what is right, only to become poor. A generous person will be enriched, and the one who gives a drink of water will receive water."

(Proverbs 11:24-25)

6. https://marathondh.com/glossary/

What's That Smell?

It all started with a whiff. You know . . . the faint smell that just isn't right when you open the door to the car. For me, it happened during those days when any and everything perishable that can fit into the hand of a two-year-old can and will end up under the driver's seat. Being a courageous young father, I swept my hand under the floorboard. Nothing. The good thing about these odors is that they're usually small enough that after a few hours, the subtle stench will be overtaken by the pine tree shaped car air freshener dangling from the rearview mirror.

Day two. The malodorous presence seemed stronger. Before heading to work, I cased the sedan, spending a good bit of time following my nose around the car. I saw nothing. I was late for work, so I let it ride. Literally.

After a week, I opened the door, and I could almost *see* the smell escaping from the car as I got in. It smelled like the car of a serial killer, and I began to fear being pulled over in rush hour traffic surrounded by police dogs and news crews. I WANTED TO SELL THE CAR! That's how desperate I was to get away from that odoriferous siege of the senses. *What's that awful smell?* After days of pure agony as I tried to find the source of stink, I finally remembered Sunday. With one kid on my hip and another at my thigh at the local seafood restaurant, I had placed a doggy bag with a full serving of lobster linguini and crab legs in the trunk. I can't begin to describe the science experiment I observed when I popped the trunk a week later! I opened the takeout box, and I'm pretty sure I saw it move!

It reminded me of marriage. Hang with me here. Not that marriage stinks, but if you're not attentive to the odor of resentment and the whiff of careless words that you speak into your relationship, the stink begins to grow. No matter how rushed life becomes, you must survey the landscape of the relationship and replay with your spouse the words and actions that were the source of the stink. If that's where you are, DO NOT SELL THE MARRIAGE! Follow your nose as long as it takes before others notice the funk inside your home. There's no can of air freshener that can mask the smell of a rotten disagreement. But you'll be amazed how quickly the aroma changes when you get the junk out of the trunk.

Oh-No Admonition

"One who loves to offend loves strife; one who builds a high threshold invites injury. One with a twisted mind will not succeed, and one with deceitful speech will fall into ruin."

(Proverbs 17:19-20)

Matt Tullos

It's Actually Better than the Movies

Husbands contend with a lot of competition. And I'm not talking about real people in a real world. I'm talking about the actors and storylines of romantic movies. Every now and then I have brief moments of romantic utterances worthy of a Nicholas Sparks movie megastar, but most of the time I sound more like John Madden. These sculpted men have the unfair competitive edge of perfect teeth, poetic conversation, and deft soundtracks fading in with impeccable timing and crafted scripts. I'm left with body spray, a ten-year-old Honda Civic, and clothes that she's already seen me wear on more than one hundred other special occasions.

Problems are also a problem. Rom-coms waltz through impossible scenarios and incredible odds with the ease of a Bolshoi ballerina. Darlene simply must contend with my two left feet. Most of our issues aren't solved in ninety minutes in the classic Hollywood formula. As a couple, we plan our romantic trysts amidst poorly timed IBS flair-ups, adolescent drama, malfunctioning ear-piercing smoke detectors, and frequent invasive medical procedures. And, of course, none of these things appear in any movie featuring Orlando Bloom, Colin Farrell, or Ryan Gosling. It's not fair. All the great lines have already been taken.

"Here's looking at you, kid"—*Casablanca*.
"I wanted it to be you; I wanted it to be you so badly"—*You've Got Mail*.
"You should be kissed, and often, and by someone who knows how"—*Gone with the Wind*.
"You make me want to be a better man"—*As Good as it Gets*.

I can't use any of those! Again . . . not fair.

But don't get me wrong. We have our moments. They're romantic moments in the midst of our ragamuffin, bed head, leaky-roof days. These moments don't need a John Williams movie score. They are richer and deeper than formulaic plotlines with predictable bow-tied resolutions. They happen when we look back and number our days filled with random rediscoveries and recommitments of our everything-ness: fishing trips, poetry, little league football, sudden everyday rescues, secret weekend rendezvous, surprise romantic moments during power outages, unbridled laughter, tears of sorrow and joy, secrets held between two of one flesh, and a thousand other things that come with a lifetime of connection. No, it's not like it is in the movies. It's so much better.

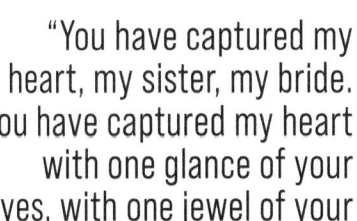

Glory Be Declaration

"You have captured my heart, my sister, my bride. You have captured my heart with one glance of your eyes, with one jewel of your necklace."

(Song of Solomon 4:9)

What's with the Rope?

Every marriage has a rope. We hide it in the closet, we carry it in the trunk of the car, or we hang it decoratively in front of the living room. It's metaphorical, but it's there, and when things get chaotic, the husband and wife pick up their end of the rope and begin to pull as hard as they can. It's a sport as old as Solomon, and even as you read these words, millions of couples are tugging away at it. Sometimes the tugging sounds like this:

-You just had to buy those shoes, didn't you?
-Who's going to stop me?
-I am! You need discipline!
-You need to lighten up!
-Oh, yeah?
-Yeah. You are obsessed with your budget.
-Well, maybe I wouldn't be obsessed with the budget if you weren't so obsessed with spending every single dime that comes into this house.

Does any of this tugging sound familiar? Sometimes it's not even the words that we say. We are tugging, yanking, squeezing, and straining, even if we don't say exactly what we mean. We code. We jab. We hint.

-Can't you control our son?!
-Would you lighten up on him? He's just five!
-He needs responsibility.
-Nurturing is what he needs.
-He gets it.
-No, he doesn't, at least not from you.
-I don't want him to grow up spoiled.
-I don't want him to grow up unloved.
-Love is tough; love is disciplined.

When you listen, I mean really listen, it all sounds a little childish, doesn't it?

-If you'd put down the remote!
-If you'd pull your weight!
-If you'd use the vacuum!
-If you'd really listen!

If you'd have some fun!
If you'd put down the iPad!
If you'd shut down your Facebook!
If you'd take some leadership!
If you'd follow my leadership!
If you'd forget the past!
If you'd plan ahead!

Like that old Gallic game of tug-o-war, somebody always gets pulled into the mud pit—muddy, miffed, and mystified. Perhaps when we notice the rope appearing in between us, we should have a different kind of dialogue. Maybe it should go something like this:

You: Hey, is this yours?
Wife: Nope. Where'd it come from?
You: I don't know. It just kind of showed up in the kitchen.
Wife: Come to think of it, I saw it the other day in our bedroom.
You: That's strange.
Wife: What should we do with it?
You: You know, you could get on one end, I could get on the other, and we could . . .
Wife: See who wins?
You: Come to think of it, sounds kind of childish.
Wife: I think I'd rather stay on your side.

Amid exhaustion and deadlines and the hurried storms of the day to day; through frustrations and disappointments, breakdowns, and plumbing catastrophes; in the midst of parenting and paying bills—we can walk in forgiveness and grace. That's how our attitude should be. Not a tug of war but a flood of grace, getting on the same side and across from the problem, not each other. When we do that, the passion returns. And then the rope is gone!

Aha Moment

"Blessed are the peacemakers, for they will be called sons of God."
(Matthew 5:9)

Three Marriage Rules to Break

I recently ran into someone I knew in college at the mall in my hometown. John was THE DUDE on campus. He married the campus beauty and received an assistantship at a prestigious law school in the northeast, which allowed him to return home and begin a successful law office. Amazingly, he remembered me. (I wasn't THE dude. I was a lower case "dude.") We decided to grab some coffee and catch up for a minute or two. He told me about his practice and his amazing house and two kids. And I couldn't help but notice the gaping hole in his story. What about his wife—that amazing wife he married shortly after we graduated? I didn't remember her name. Seems like it started with a *J*. Do I ask, or do I leave town with this question bothering me for days? I thought, *What will it hurt to ask this guy about his wife?* So with as much ease and casual grace as I could muster, I asked, "So how's, um . . . Jane doing?"

"Jill?"

"Right! Jill."

John took a deep breath. "We split after the second baby. She wanted way too much from me. I felt smothered, and my personality just wasn't connecting with hers. Jill was impossible. She got upset when she didn't know where all my money was going. She constantly questioned my schedule. If I was a few hours late or had to stay at the office overnight without telling her, she'd freak. And she became very paranoid when I struck up friendships with the opposite sex. I felt like she assumed she married an *Amish* guy who signed an agreement *not* to have a life."

This was an uncomfortable situation for me. I dislike people who judge others as much as anybody, but I had huge alarms going off in my head. How could someone so smart be so far adrift in the ocean of relationships and marriage? The three objections that he mentioned in his terse explanation created the perfect storm, which led to a bankruptcy, joint custody, and many complicated, awkward conversations, like the one we were having. You see, John had some rules about his life and his marriage. These marriage rules must be broken if your marriage is going to be everything you, your spouse, and God desires it to be. By all means, let your freak flag fly and break these idiotic rules our culture values.

Your money is your money. Many couples I counsel fail to recognize that marriage is a financial partnership. God wants you and your spouse to work together, and He's quite interested in the way you manage money in your marriage. It's a tool God uses to teach us about sacrifice, unconditional love, communication, cooperation, trust, and stewardship. We learn these virtues in the classroom of finances. The idea of separating the money that comes into the home is a dubious proposal. Leave a legacy of growth and sacrifice by working together as a family to achieve financial decisions and goals.

Your time is your time. Every person needs time to be alone. It's essential for prayer, reflection, and restoration of mind and body. But to assume that *your* time is *your* time is to miss the entire message of a covenant marriage. I know, you're busy. But you're married too! Your time is no longer *just* your time. We have to learn balance. If you don't have balance in your schedule, find it! If you are making decisions alone regarding your time, your marriage can become toxic fast. The issue of time and money can present the greatest threats to your marriage. Remember: the best barometers of your love for your spouse and your love of God are *money* and *time*. In fact, Jesus felt so strongly about these two life values that He spent more time on them than He did on anything else.

Your friends are your friends. (In other words, there should be no problem at all with husbands having a close female friend or two; and the same is true for wives about a male friend.) This is a rule that often leads to sticky, complicated messes. John held on to this rule with white knuckles until his marriage imploded. He fell for a client with whom he spent lots of time. What began as an innocent working relationship grew into emotional cheating. One may begin a relationship as functional allies. It may begin with an innocent compliment then giving way to subtle flirtations, discussing marriage trouble, gift giving, sharing meals, and traveling in the same cars. And once that train leaves the station, it's difficult to stop. Don't trust your heart enough to do these things. Run away from these opportunities! Nothing good happens when you go there.

And the story continues . . . .

So that's the story of a friend of mine who didn't break these insidious rules and broke his marriage in the process. In fact, he married the client. Happily married today? No. Believe it or not, she had the same issues with John's rules as wife number one. They split less than a year after their marriage began. It's the story of so many divorces: couples who were madly in love but refused to break some rules to save their marriage.

Oh-No Admonition

"A fool does not delight in understanding, but only wants to show off his opinions."

(Proverbs 18:2)

Oh-No, Aha, and Glory Be

Matt Tullos

Playing by the Rules

I have a friend who grew up in Africa and has no understanding or interest in football. He just doesn't get it. Just like I don't get soccer (or as he calls it, "real football"). If I step back a little, I can understand why. There are so many different rules, penalties, and strategies. Our referees have microphones, but they don't explain things for the new viewers. It's like a language Americans pick up as kids and take for granted after years of watching it.

Marriage is like that. If you weren't around marriage all your life, there are a lot of things you wouldn't understand, like, *Why's that guy sitting by himself, holding a purse outside a ladies' dressing room in the women's apparel section of a department store?* If you didn't know anything about marriage, it would confuse you.

The closest thing we have to a rule book on marriage is the Bible. God sets up the guidelines of healthy marriages, but He also gives us a number of cautionary examples which communicate, *For goodness sakes, don't do it like that guy in Genesis* (or Exodus, Ecclesiastes, Acts, and almost every other book in the Bible). There are other practical rules husbands and wives set up that aren't morally complex. They just make for a happy marriage. Here are a few:

Illegal procedure: We have lots of illegal procedures in our home. I don't go to bed without locking the doors. I don't watch ahead on shows we are currently binge watching together. And there's a certain way my wife wants me to fold my socks. For the life of me, I don't understand it, but for some reason it's important to her. To do otherwise would be an illegal procedure.

False start: That's when I act like I'm going to do something my wife asked me to do, and then I get distracted. For me, this happens often. That's a false start. I'm notorious for false starts.

Pass interference is when I totally ruin romantic moments with a joke or order a dish with lots of garlic or look at my phone when she's talking. These are buzz-kills when she's about to make a pass at me. And I hate it when the penalty is enforced!

And there are other infractions. *Personal fouls* are when I get super critical. *Offsides?* That's when I roll over in bed and accidentally elbow her in the ribs. *Illegal substitution* is when I get snippy because I was treated unjustly at work by the boss. *Tripping* is when I think that I've won an argument. Winning an argument in marriage? If you think that is *ever* a good thing, you are obviously tripping!

Finally, if a call is *controversial*, we always send the dispute up to God for review. He always gets the call right.

Oh-No Admonition

"Seek to lead a quiet life, to mind your own business, and to work with your own hands, as we commanded you, so that you may behave properly in the presence of outsiders and not be dependent on anyone."

(1 Thessalonians 4:11-12)

A (Very Personal) Glory Be

In 1986, we walked out that door at Lake Arlington Baptist Church.

We had no idea what an adventure we would encounter.

Ratty apartments.

Youth camps.

Seminary papers.

Four boys, breathtaking ministry experiences, mission trips, interstate thunderstorm spin-outs, traveling, teaching, and sixteen abodes.

We've gone through the roller coaster of the minister's home. We've had opportunities to serve at conferences and with publishers. Lots of ball games with the guys and late night church crises and breakthroughs. We've prayed together, laughed together, wept together, and had our share of tragedy and disappointments.

Satan has, more than a few times, gotten all up in our business, but we're still standing together. Darlene has taught me so much about life, and I am so glad we didn't give up on each other during difficult times. She's helped me find keys, wallets, and rental trucks. You see, the beauty married a dyslexic ragamuffin. She has put up with my inability to say no, my codependency, and my bouts with depression. And I'm thankful we're still under the same roof as comrades, friends, and lovers in this scattered feast called life. I'm thankful for all the friends and churches who taught us how to be married. There would be no way to mention them all, but you know who you are, and we owe so much to you.

We aren't perfect. Marriage reminds us of that fact every day, doesn't it? It's a lot easier to pull off "impressive" when you don't share a bathroom with anybody. Marriage is a blessing, but it is also God's spotlight on our brokenness and need for grace. We are still learning about marriage through conferences, books, conversations, mentors, and lots of prayer. I'm so glad we are still in it together, still walking arm in arm through life—for better or for worse, in sickness and in health, til death do us part.

Glory Be Declaration

"Give thanks to the Lord, for he is good. His love endures forever."

(Psalm 143:1)

PART 3:
Parenting

Oh-No: I thought I'd be a model dad, but I have absolutely no idea what I'm doing anymore.
Aha: These kids are so much like me!
Glory Be: Through fatherhood, I'm learning to be more like Him!

I guess I never really grasped the enormity of the task. The twenty-four-hour-ness of the job. It's a great job. Indeed, it is the most invigorating, mind bending, spiritually challenging job ever invented. But there was so much I didn't know.

Oh-No, Aha, and Glory Be

That's Normal

It's late July. The final days are upon us when we turn our attention away from having kids 24/7. While visions of school buses dance in the heads of many parents, they are definitely ready. It was a long haul in the Covid days of 2020–2021. Most parents spent so many days struggling through Zoom™ school, sudden closings, and that weird season of the pandemic called *Covid-cabin fever*. The symptoms were pretty universal: incessant Zoom lessons, Wi-Fi crashes, unending *Floor Is Lava* games, and online counseling for the parents and grandparents who have served as the ringmasters.

But what is normal anyway?

It's been so long that you may have forgotten. Allow me to remind you. Normal is when you make it a whole week without having to run back to the school at 10 a.m. to deliver the lunch money you forgot to send with your famished fourth grader. Normal is when your eighth grader's entire world is irreparably falling apart because the woman of his dreams is now "dating" the quarterback, and he will never *ever* recover to love again for the rest of his life, and he *really* doesn't want to talk about it. *Really*.

Normal is when you've got a dance recital and a basketball game at the same time, and your daughter and son think you love the other sibling more. Normal is when everybody else knows how the carpool line works, except your husband who gets busted dropping your daughter off in the faculty parking lot. Normal is when you get that sinking feeling that your kids will be permanently scarred by subtle flaws and mindless moments. It keeps you up at night thinking that somebody will find out that the thing your kid is struggling with is because you aren't as hard core as Dr. Phil, as gentle and loving as Mr. Rogers, as spiritually connected as Max Lucado, or as macho as Dwayne "The Rock" Johnson. Normal is when you look at your kids and you realize that you love them so much that you hug them a little too long and a little too hard.

Normal is when you see them succeeding, growing, and thriving, and you wonder how you could be so blessed to have them, despite all your wrong turns, missed opportunities, bad advice, and inherited flaws. Actually, that's the part that's *not* normal. That's the part that's amazing.

Glory Be Declaration

"Because of the Lord's faithful love we do not perish, for his mercies never end. They are new every morning; great is your faithfulness! I say, 'The Lord is my portion, therefore I will put my hope in him.'"

(Lamentations 3:22-24)

Matt Tullos

A Dozen Things I've Learned from Boys

As the father of four sons, I've picked up a lot of life experiences, and I understand much more about the journey to manhood than I did when I began. Here are a dozen things I learned in the process:

1. There are a million types of odors that can emit from their bedrooms, cars, and duffle bags. One day with my guys could send a bloodhound into shock and awe.
2. Their competitive nature can spring forth in almost any sort of daily experience, from car seat assignments, trampoline brawls, frog populations in their bedrooms, and superpowers they are convinced they have.
3. They have more words for *gas* than Eskimos have words for *snow*.
4. In a matter of one day, during puberty they go from inappropriate nakedness at the drop of a hat to the sudden modesty of an Amish elder.
5. Unlike the girls, when it comes to the young boys, clothes are no big deal. Just make sure the five-year-old doesn't get creative and wear his underwear over his pants.
6. Another note about apparel: always, *always* check the pockets before washing. Pockets are usually the storage and filing compartments for all types of boy stuff that can ruin the clothes or ruin the washing machine—or both.
7. Boys have no concept of time. When they are in time-out for five minutes, it is the equivalent of a presidential term. If it is a day at the amusement park, after ten hours, they "just got there."
8. The boys, I have discovered, are far more gullible than the girls. They easily accept bigfoot sightings, zombie apocalypses, UFOs, and the existence of organic jelly beans.
9. For boys, unlimited soft serve ice cream is the closest they will come to a spiritual experience before the age of accountability. It's so unbelievable that their brains can't process the idea.
10. Emergency rooms are an unavoidable destination (and you'll be back . . . again . . . and again). They will go there, and so will you, with stories and explanations that will seem impossible to you even though you, yourself, witnessed the feat of daring they attempted.
11. Unlike in the movies, animals *will* be harmed in the raising of this child. Boys don't intentionally harm or torture them. And the animals *usually* survive. But there are just certain things boys want to try out. They learn that large dogs should not be ridden as horses, and pillowcases don't work well as cat parachutes when catapulted from the roof of the house.
12. In the end, boys do grow up, and you'll have a lifetime of stories to tell. You'll also learn to love the permanent marker dinosaur drawings on your white leather couch.

Oh-No Admonition

"Do not despise the Lord's instruction, my son, and do not loathe his discipline; for the Lord disciplines the one he loves, just as a father disciplines the son in whom he delights."

(Proverbs 3:11-12)

He Was 5' 23"

My grandfather was five feet, twenty-three inches tall. Actually, he was well under six feet, but he was a giant, legendary figure. I grew up during my preschool days in Los Angeles. As a knee-high kid, my brother and I would fly to spend several weeks in Dry Prong, Louisiana. Dry Prong is near Tioga. Don't know Tioga? Let's just say that Dry Prong built the boondocks located in Tioga. Dry Prong couldn't afford boondocks. We loved our time out in the sticks learning about possums, grasshoppers, cow pies, mosquito nets, feather beds, and fireflies.

We learned a new dialect. *Far* was pronounced *fur*. Cool Whip™ was *cool werp*. And *tar* could mean anything from, "I've got a flat tar," to "Doesn't our town have a great-looking water tar?"

We called my grandfather Goodbuddy. He had an eighth grade education and a small farm in the sticks of rural central Louisiana. I still have old reel-to-reel recordings he would mail to Mom and Dad during our longer visits. I love hearing him say my name on those tapes. "Matthew's a good little boy. Got him trained to the outside and the hose." Interpretation: *He taught me that I didn't need to come inside to use the bathroom or get a drink.*

He was introverted, but he had plenty of stories. Funny ones. Most involved the usual suspects: his oil field bunkhouse mates, my dad, my grandmother, and the ten or so dogs that he programed to hate raccoons with the fire of a thousand suns.

I have a few stories on him as well. I remember the last conversation we had with him in the hospital. I asked him where my seventy-two-year-old grandmother was. His classic response was, "She's gone to the beauty shop. She never gives up."

He was country, but he hated country music—or as he called it, "honky-tonkin" music. He said it like he was cussing. In fact, I was around thirteen before I realized you could say "honky-tonk" in public.

He wasn't the best at formal, public prayer, but he did pray. There are more than a few stories of him lying face down in the middle of his pasture, praying before the dawn. This made him taller than most. He taught me how to eat sardines with saltine crackers, how and when to spit, how to shake a hand firmly, how to make a lady feel important, and how to keep my mouth shut when I didn't know what I was talking about. And to have the temperament of a pit bull when it came to defending children.

He was the kind of man that loved everybody, but grandkids were in a class by themselves. I don't have grandkids. I'm praying I'll get to have some in the future. I will be an awesome grandfather. I was trained by the best.

Glory Be Declaration

"May the Lord our God be with us as he was with our ancestors. May he not abandon us or leave us."

(1 Kings 8:57)

Matt Tullos

Honey, I Shrunk My Underwear!

I seem to underestimate the amount of stuff I need when I go out of town. Packing is always the last thing I think about, which means I'm usually scrambling around in the dark at 4:30 a.m. before the flight. I just throw things in a duffle bag. No lists, no lights, no strategy, and no regrets. (Well, that last part is not exactly true. I often have *lots* of regrets when I get to where I'm going.) There's always something that I forget to bring. I unzip my vintage Michael Jordan duffle bag and realize a little too late that I didn't pack razors or socks or deodorant or the right underwear. Back when my sons were little, I accidently grabbed a stack of freshly folded tighty-whities off the sofa. What a mistake! They were my eight-year-old son's underwear instead of my own. They were tighty-whities, just like mine. But they were a boy's size ten. Needless to say, it was an excruciating day leading conferences in rural Colorado before I could leave camp to procure logically fitting undergarments. I guess you could say they brought new meaning to "tighty-whity."

My wife is just the opposite: packing starts days in advance with three extra outfits per day. She brings it *all*. The contrast is as stunning as the difference between a storage trunk on wheels and a brown paper bag. We balance each other out between the two diametrically positioned virtues of traveling light and being prepared in season and out of season. Both packing strategies—my *last-minute-throw-it-in-as-fast-as-you-can* strategy and my wife's *bring-everything-because-you-just-never-know* strategy—are a study in marital contrasts that provides lots of growth opportunities.

I'm learning that poor planning and limited prep time means precarious predicaments. And my wife is learning that substantially stuffed suitcases sometimes create super-strenuous situations for her sidekick.

Darlene and I are sharpening each other, knowing that all growth involves change. We fill in each other's gaps and teach each other new grooves every day. The writer of Hebrews writes, "Jesus Christ is the same yesterday, today and forever." Jesus is perfect and completely sufficient. I'm not, so I need to change. Especially when it comes to underwear during a week-long conference in the Rockies.

Oh-No Admonition

"When I was a child, I spoke like a child, I thought like a child, I reasoned like a child. When I became a man, I put aside childish things."

(1 Corinthians 13:11)

The Flood

It was the great flood of 2010 in Nashville, Tennessee. The weather guy said it was a one in one thousand year flood. Whew! Glad we got that over with. That's the way I often look at difficult things. God is in control, and we had it coming. It's a twisted view of reality. I'm astounded by how quickly my mind always begins to hyper-personalize those "acts of God."

I sloshed into my basement and was somewhat relieved that we really didn't have much damage. But still, it was difficult to wrap my brain around thirteen inches in thirty hours. That's crazy! Like millions of Tennesseans, by the time our family realized that we had a flood coming our way, we simply didn't have enough lumber for the ark. And the animals weren't showing up two by two. By way of animals, we only had a cat, and he was spayed. Even the ducks in the park seemed traumatized as they stumbled onto a major thoroughfare, gawking at the swollen lake like a toddler at the edge of the pool. It would seem to me that the water would give them a sense of home field advantage over humans, but they looked at the rising waters as if to say, *I've lost so much!*

Just about every church in the area began the hard work of ripping out carpets in homes and collecting debris and mattresses. One of my friends remarked about the scene at the Opryland Hotel and the mall, which used to be an amusement park: "It's like the log ride is operational again but with cleaner water." When I got back home from a three-hour traffic jam, the smell of our basement told me that we had a lot of work to do, even though we didn't get nearly the amount of damage as most. The air conditioner gasped its final breath, and the house smelled like a crockpot of gym socks. I was tired, hot, and mechanically challenged. When I get into situations like these and feel out of control, I have a tendency to heighten the passion with which I do stuff. It's what we pessimistic stuffers do when we fall back into original sin. I began my ballet of disgust by slinging wet boxes on top of each other and making crazy decisions, like trying to place the ping pong table on the top of a riding mower. This provided great entertainment for my sons. I also cussed a blue streak with my own made-up words: "Clamping tar mink baby rick rack!" (Is it a sin to have my own set of personal vulgarities? I think so.)

Nathan came down the stairs into the basement. I didn't hear him, and there I was, in all my pessimistic glory, in cutoffs, a t-shirt, and old dress shoes. (I didn't want to get my white sneakers tainted.)

"Uhh . . . so, Dad. Do you need some help?"

"No. I'm good," I said. "I'm just a little fed up with all this stuff. We've been doing the Dave Ramsey thing, and we can all say a bon voyage to the emergency fund I'd been building up."

Nathan switched roles with me and became the comforting father, providing levity despite the broken levies. "I think it's great! You've always prayed that God would give you ministry opportunities, and they're everywhere. Maybe this was an act of God to really let us see what's really important."

Whoa, whoa, whoa . . . is this the son who thought the world was coming to an end when his prom date got chicken pox? Amazing.

Nathan continued: "Plus, all these boxes and things are down here because they didn't rate a place on the main floor. It's just stuff. And with all the extra room we gain from this, we might even be able to do something really cool down here. Besides, this isn't gonna happen for another thousand years." After a few more minutes of conversation with my teenage son, I realized how blessed I am to have a son who can get me back in the proper frame of mind. He's like my personal restart button.

After about an hour, I found the solution to the air conditioning problem. (A minor miracle for a dad who barely knows how to adjust the thermostat.) We salvaged what we could and went to the church to begin another expedition to help those who had it a *lot* worse than we did.

I am reminded that kids can often coach parents—when we are open to really listen. There have been times when one of our four boys offered some painful truth telling and very sage-like advice. Caleb, at the age of four, once said to me, "Dad, maybe you and Mom need to get out of the house more." "Good advice, Son. We do need to get out of the house and date."

I am also reminded that it's so easy for us to get so immersed in a flood of distractions, desires, emotions, and technicalities that we miss how incredibly precious every day we have with each other really is!

Aha Moment

"Lord, our Lord, how magnificent is Your name throughout the earth! You have covered the heavens with Your majesty. Because of Your adversaries, You have established a stronghold from the mouths of children."

(Psalm 8:1-2b)

Oh-no, Aha, and Glory Be

Matt Tullos

He Never Met a Stranger

Over the past few years, there's been recognition of a cultural phenomenon that has been around since Adam: the dad jokes. I'm sure Adam had a few. And they wouldn't be a fig leaf of your imagination. What is it that happens to men of a certain age? What chemical changes occur in the brain that cause this compelling need to make their children groan at a middle-aged man's punchline? I don't know, but my dad was a superstar in the dad joke sub-culture. Anyone can resort to silly puns and awkward knock-knocks. My dad's jokes had an unusual degree of difficulty to pull off.

My dad was an extreme extrovert. I've never met a man who was so energized by talking to strangers. It didn't matter who it was; he'd give them an earful of awkward entertainment, and I'm sure he scared a few people along the way. He certainly scared me when we went grocery shopping together. One day I counted. He talked to thirteen strangers and five people he knew. I'm talking one visit, and we only went there for hoagie buns. It took us *three hours*! As an extreme introvert, it drove me crazy, but people usually left his presence with a smile on their faces. Please don't try these. He was a trained professional:

"Hi! I'd like to help you out! Which way did you come in?"

"You know you ought to go to Hollywood. The walk would do you good!"

"I was born twins, and I was born at sea. My dad told my mom, 'Pick the best one, and I'll throw the other one overboard.' [Long pause.] I swam ashore."

When someone accidentally burped, he'd always, *and I mean always,* remark, "Bring it up again, and we'll vote on it."

This next one he'd say when meeting a couple. (Bless their hearts.) I heard my dad do this one on hundreds of couples. I'm not exaggerating:

"You must have dated her in the dark. [Awkward pause.] She would never have dated you in the daylight."

Surprise your next stranger with this conversation starter:

"Hey, we're related. [*Enjoy the look of confusion on their face*s. *Then continue.*] Your mother and my mother are mothers."

Now, dads, if you want to scare off your son's potential girlfriend, here's a great one-liner my dad invented:

"You know, the last girl my son dated had the most beautiful blonde hair . . . coming out of her left nostril."

Oh-No, Aha, and Glory Be

He had lots more, but as he got older, he stuck with these as his standards. He practiced on me every day.

We had other traditions. He used to call me at 5 a.m. on Easter Sunday and shout, "He's not there!" It was his way of celebrating the empty tomb. Dad's gone now. Last Easter was the first one without that phone call, but I'm sure he's making friends in heaven and adding to his repertoire of highly challenging dad jokes.

Glory Be Declaration

"Our mouths were filled with laughter then, and our tongues with shouts of joy."
(Psalm 126:2)

Matt Tullos

I Wrestle Not

I have a confession to make. Love really hurts these days. It all began when my fourteen-year-old got MMA lessons for his birthday. Often I come through the door of the house, and somewhere lurking in the shadows is a one-hundred-forty-pound guy with the body fat of a coat hanger who will bring me into submission. This was fun when he didn't know Brazilian Jujitsu. There's a lot I didn't know about MMA. It would have been great if he would have told me that "tap out" is a mercy command. I would have tapped out the moment I caught a glimpse of his swan dive from the top of the stairs to the top of my head as I came through the foyer of our home.

I've learned a few terms over the past few weeks, including . . .

The *arm bar*: a joint lock that hyperextends the elbow. Note: It causes pain. Tap out, Dad.

The *anaconda choke*: consists of trapping one of your opponent's arms with an under-hook and clasping hands on the other side of his neck, squeezing his neck and arm together to cut off air supply. Note: Anytime *anaconda* and *choke* are used in the same sentence, I don't want to be involved.

The *heel hook*: a hold which is applied on the heel and then fully accomplished by twisting the knee at the joint. (I am limping this morning.)

The *twister*: involves facing your opponent's feet while in half guard, putting your hand on your opponent's knee, and creating space to spin your foe into submission. (I prefer the Milton Bradley game version.)

There's a lot of stress for my ninth grader, and if being his personal crash test dummy creates a bond between us, I'm in. I will recover from his pinch grip ties, arm bars, over-hooks, and leg locks. Caleb is a guy, and like most guys, we are programmed for battle. I'm even more proud that he realizes that there's a spiritual battle out there and in here. I know there will come a day when he won't be hiding around the corner to see if he's stronger than his father. The connections we make together over the next four years will impact his life and mine for eternity. There's a formidable foe, and he has a strategy for both of us. We're ready. And together with God, the ultimate tap out is certain!

Oh-No Admonition

"For our struggle is not against flesh and blood, but against the rulers, against the authorities, against the cosmic powers of this darkness, against evil, spiritual forces in the heavens."

(Ephesians 6:12)

I Am Not in Charge

I set my hopes high in 1988 when I began the journey into parenthood. I read the books, listened to the tapes, and went to seminars on tough love, safety, CPR, and potty training. I went to those birthing classes provided by the local hospital; I breathed, focused, massaged, and encouraged just like the other ten men in the class did. We borrowed a real, live newborn from some friends in our Sunday school class to have a dry run at answering the phone, changing diapers, and mixing formula simultaneously. My wife was much better at that than me, by the way.

But after over ten years of experience at parenthood and four boys later, I have been tempted to ask, *Did I miss something?*

There are so many things that changed—so many things that were not mentioned by my doctor, James Dobson, Mom, certainly not Dad, the surgeon general, or Big Bird. I didn't realize that from birth until a baby was old enough to talk, I was no longer in charge. My wife was not even in charge. This fifteen-pound baby in the blue room with teddy bear wallpaper was in charge.

The agenda changed dramatically. Some nights my schedule included a 2 a.m. drive around town where I sang, "Father Abraham Had Many Sons" at least two hundred times. I'd sing it fast. I'd sing it slow. My little boy's eyes would get blinky, and I'd sing softer and softer and softer until almost inaudible, and then the moment I stopped, a sudden burst of infant rage would erupt from the car seat. And I'd begin another long version of the dreaded song. Not "Old Macdonald," not "King of the Jungle," not "Ten Little Indians," not "Itsy Bitsy Spider . . ." not even "Little Rabbit in the Woods." "Father Abraham" and "Father Abraham" alone would calm the torrent.

I was not in charge.

I didn't realize that, to my kids, I would emerge not only as the spiritual leader of the house but also as the candy police. Three-year-old boys will do just about anything to get candy. Example: I am going to the grocery store to pick up a few things for Darlene. I decide to give her a break and take the baby and our three-year-old son, Jacob. Of course, the checkout line is a plethora of sugar products. How they come up with so many packaging ideas for candy amazes me. After saying no 234 times in a three-minute span, I manage to make it through the line, pay for my groceries, load the shopping cart, and secure my dear ones to my side. (By the way, where have all the bag boys gone?) We get to the car. I use my best stern, parental commanding voice: "You stay here," I say to Jacob as I begin to strap the baby into the car seat. By the time I turn around, Jacob, who is patiently waiting for me to open his door, has already found a piece of used bubble gum on the blacktop and popped it into his mouth. I suppose you could call him a strong advocate of recycling. And of course, I do my well-rehearsed parental gross-out jig and remove it. I thought I had won the candy war, but at that moment I realized the truth.

Again, I was not in charge.

Matt Tullos

I didn't realize that there would be so many jars, and wipes, and tubes, and tools involved in the child rearing process. I remember one of those nights when I tried to rush the parental responsibilities along. It was a night when I didn't think I would collapse from exhaustion the moment we got our kids to bed. Who knows, Darlene might be up for a little romance. So with an extra burst of energy, I quickly bathed the kids, washed their hair, gave the third son the magic ear infection pink stuff, and then began to brush their teeth. But something was wrong. I brushed, but there was no foam. I quickly looked at the tube that I presumed was the toothpaste and screamed: "Diaper rash ointment!" You know—the sticky white stuff. "I wondered why it wasn't foaming up!" The lady manning the poison control hotline was cordial, but I think she could have handled the situation a little more professionally. I could hear her try to muffle the phone as she said, "Louise! Louise! You gotta hear this one! The guy brushed his kid's teeth with zinc oxide!"

I guess I never really grasped the enormity of the task. The twenty-four-hour-ness of the job. It's a great job. Indeed, it is the most invigorating, mind-bending, spiritually challenging job ever invented. But there was so much I didn't know.

Now with four boys, I can't remember the last time I ordered a meal for myself at McDonald's. I now understand that I can subsist on the leftover French fries and half eaten chicken nuggets. So this is what I've become—a bag man with a master's degree.

The other night I found myself eating ice cream in the closet. I've become very adept at treat smuggling. Because, as all parents know, if you are seen dipping out some ice cream for yourself, you're going to be dipping a whole lot more before the night is over.

Even in entertainment I come up short:

- My Frank Capra movie collection: three
- The kids' sing-along video library: fifty-three

But would we trade our wacky, adventurous life, raising four boys, three gerbils, two dogs, an iguana, and a stressed-out cat? Not for a second. We have our moments, but we can never thank God enough for how He's raising us as we raise our kids. The boys are doing great, despite my parental bloopers, oversights, and eccentricities. They have all their limbs. They haven't poked their eyes out. They are robust and full of dreams. God is in control, and as I write, they are all sleeping like angelic masterpieces. But they will wake up in a few hours, and the fun will begin again. But thankfully God is in control.

And I am *definitely* not in charge.

Glory Be Declaration

"When I am afraid, I will trust in you. In God, whose word I praise, in God I trust; I will not be afraid. What can mere mortals do to me?"

(Psalm 56:3-4)

Oh-No, Aha, and Glory Be

I'm Just Sayin . . .
The Power of a Parent's Rants, Promises, and Praise

I have a confession to make. My four sons have created a lexicon of the most wrong-headed rants and phrases that I've said. Now that they're all in their teens, they entertain each other with these stories. They don't remember the great pearls of wisdom that I toss casually along their path when my quiet times transform me into a hybrid of Beth Moore, Oswald Chambers, and Billy Graham. They rarely remember the times when I precisely calculated the family budget, when I fixed bikes with bailing wire and a discarded bra strap from my wife's closet, or my keen ability to recall the answer to fourth grade history questions without googling. They do, however, remember my thunderous rants about bunk bed safety, sanitary conditions in the bathroom, and driving instruction (i.e., "Whoa . . . WHOA! WHOA! WHOA! WHOA!"). These parental sermons of mine gave birth to a kind of parental gibberish. I'm not proud of these moments.

One of their favorite games is to catch me stealing lines of dramatic dialogue from an old movie as I debate curfew, dog cruelty, or church attendance.

"Dad, that sounds like *Rocky 3*—Mr. T." They all laugh, including my wife. Yes, I've been busted for argumentative improvisational plagiarism by an eleven-year-old movie buff.

Sometimes I forget that not everyone shared the same legends and traditions as I did.

"Look at this room! It looks like Gilly Williams' place!"

"Gilly Williams?" My thirteen-year-old isn't as used to the term as the older brothers.

Gilly Williams was a guy who squatted on my great-grandfather's land back in the 40s. Gilly lived in so much squalor that his name has been passed down generationally in my family as the ultimate illustration of messiness. But without hearing the legend, I suppose my simile held little to no meaning to a son whose room really did look like an a-bomb testing site (or like Gilly Williams' place). I should have gone with the a-bomb testing site imagery.

And so I submit to you a handful of lessons I've learned the hard way . . . and I'll try not to recreate movie dialogue to make my point.

But Dad! You promised! Sometimes I've made the mistake of prioritizing people in order of their weight. The big people get priority first. That leaves my kids at a distinct disadvantage. Jacob was just six years old when he felt the pain of being outweighed. I had promised him that after I completed an important project, we'd go see a movie he'd been looking forward to seeing since he saw the trailer a few months earlier. He'd ask me about it almost every morning. Bleary eyed from the late nights trying to change the world and impress my boss, I'd explain that I had more to do before I'd have a night free. The project at work lasted a couple of days longer than the movie's run. I tried to redeem the situation, but I should have noticed how selfish my priorities had become. I was promising far too much to "big people." The project at work impressed my boss but didn't make the cut when it was proposed to company management. I regret the choice I made because life became all about my job and not the higher calling of being a dad. The book of Proverbs underscores this truth with this warning: *It is a trap for anyone to dedicate something rashly and later to reconsider his vows* (Proverbs 20:25 HCSB).

Do you remember a time when your mom or dad didn't keep a promise? Did they ever apologize? If not, change the spiritual landscape by keeping promises. Promises are great rewards but horrible motivators. If you keep your promises, you are saying to your kids, *You can trust me. My words have value and meaning.* If you don't, you'll lose something very sacred, and you'll spend a huge amount of energy and time trying to restore their trust.

Practice the power of a sincere apology. Isn't it uncomfortable when you are in a debate with your child, and their side begins to make more sense than yours? It feels embarrassing. Aren't parents always supposed to win the argument? The old rule of parenting is that parents are never wrong, and if they are wrong, they should never apologize.

My two oldest sons celebrated the twenty-first-century rite of passage a few years back: a cell phone. It was 2004, when phones flipped and passcodes were nonexistent. We found one of those family plans where you get four phones and four numbers on one plan. That Friday night, I called my oldest son's number. The line was busy. Every time I tried to call, the line continued to go to a voicemail that wasn't set up yet. The longer I tried, the more frustrated I became. When he finally got home, I was furious. I had no idea what he was trying to pull, but I knew it had to be something. Face red, eyes bulging from the sockets, I articulated the longest run-on sentence in the long sad history of parental lectures. Then he looked at me and calmly said, "You picked up the wrong phone. The one you gave me was your phone. The one that I have is your phone. You've been calling *yourself*!"

Oh-No, Aha, and Glory Be

Oops. A sincere apology was in order.

One of the biggest gripes I hear from students that have broken, dysfunctional, and generally messed up relationships is that their parents were unable to admit mistakes. Our desire to be the perfect, spotless, infallible one really blocks their path to the real Messiah. Therefore, asking for forgiveness can be one of the most powerful, game-changing feats of parenting. When we never fess up to our huge failures and/or subtle peccadilloes, we become a source of frustration and despair. For many, this swims against the current of our family history. We grew up in homes where we just didn't question. When we experienced a mess, it was hidden or dismissed with petty excuse. We fast-forward twenty years, and as parents, we are hard-wired to sweep our parental sins under the rug. It's a major cog in the machine of generational sins. The only way to stop it is to speak it, as painful or as humiliating as it sometimes is, especially for men.

Don't focus on the don'ts. Many parents have a three-word mission statement for their kid: "Don't mess up." We get so focused on crime and punishment that life steals the joy out of parenting. Let's remind each other to catch our kids doing something right. This takes some practice since some of us grew up in homes where words of praise were few. This doesn't mean drown them in praise. The best way to see results is by noticing their accomplishments and coaching them for better success. If you see something you'd like your child to improve on, first notice what they're doing right, and then give them some adjustment on how they can improve. Praise your child with your voice, your eye contact, your expression, and your hands!

I've been amazed to see how much better my kids respond to my parenting when I first affirm their effort and what they're doing right. If your child comes home with all As and Bs and one D in algebra, where does the focus of your parenting naturally gravitate? Of course it's to that D in algebra. Certainly we have to help our kids focus on areas of improvement, but don't forget the areas of strength. Don't let the D steal all the joy of God-given excellence in the other five classes. Don't forget to praise and offer unconditional acceptance of your child as a unique person with huge areas of strength.

*Besides, algebra . . . what's that all about? Numbers mixed with letters? Something's wrong about that. I'm just saying.

Grow up with your kids. I'm convinced that one of the reasons God gives us kids is to keep us in a state of constant accountability, reality, and growth. Not much gets by them, does it? Even two-year-olds have an uncanny and sometimes maddening ability to scrape away the veneer of happy-shiny appearance management and bring us into the realm of seeing our true messiness. Sometimes our lives spin out of control. Inside—deep down—we are a wreck equal to Gilly Williams' place. They get that. So we as parents have a choice. We can hide our messiness, or we can confess it in front of them and let them know that we are still growing, changing, and learning in a myriad of ways. The airport adage is important: *Put on your own oxygen mask before you assist your children.*

The implications of growing up are huge. We can stay with the familiar patterns of how we deal with relationships, parenting, and emotional pain . . . or, we can grow into something real, powerful, and transformational. So where do I start? That was my question a few years ago when I faced some substantial nosedives into the canyon of parental shame, marital meltdowns, and deep disappointments. Personally, I think you've already started. You've made it to the end of this article! Now connect with others in the community. This pilgrimage isn't for lone rangers. Most Christians refuse to be in a transparent small group. It could be a support group or a small group or even a ministry team. Find a safe place to connect, and then live out your life in front of your children. Grow, forgive, receive forgiveness, and, if you're married, as far as it depends upon you, stay married and work God's plan out in your relationship. Keep your marital slate clean. It's hard work. But it's good work.

Oh-No Admonition

"If possible, as far as it depends on you, live at peace with everyone."
(Romans 12:18)

Oh-no, Aha, and Glory Be

84

There's No Such Thing as "Just a Mom"

Last Thursday, I was behind a lady at the grocery store. It's a national chain, but not one of those fancy all organic places where they offer free samples of tofu ice cream and sushi. It's the "bag your own stuff" kind of place where you can buy enough beans to feed the French resistance at a deep discount. She had a baby on her hip, one in the cart, and three right beside her. She was a professional. She carried more coupons than I've ever seen. Totally organized. By the time she finished checking out and redeeming her coupons, I thought they were going to have to pay her for taking the groceries. It was really close. In the middle of this important and somewhat shadowy financial transaction, she also managed to tamp down a sibling mutiny between two of her toddlers, convince a twelve-year-old that chocolate causes acne, and give a plausible explanation to an eight-year-old for fake UFO sightings printed on the *National Enquire* nearby. I was in awe. This lady had it going on in the "Mom department." It reminded me of how difficult mothering can be, if done right.

Being a mom requires a ton of multitasking and lots of counterbalancing. To be a good mom, you must have the patience of Job, the wisdom of Solomon, the compassion of Mother Teresa, the financial savvy of Warren Buffet, and the defensive prowess of Chuck Norris, all in the same day.

I've seen a mom settle a dispute with a single sentence. Of course, the tone and volume of that sentence may have had a little to do with it. A mom can ease a pain with a kiss on the affected area. I've never pulled that one off successfully. I've tried.

My wife can handle and clean up just about anything except for vomit. I am chairman of the vomit department at our house. She has a sensitive gag reflex. Just about everything else she can handle just fine, thank you very much. Sincerely, Dear . . . *thank you very much.*

I'm also grateful that I'm the designated driver on long trips. That seems to be a universal agreement in most families. The dude drives. I'm not a better driver, but someone has to drive while negotiations worthy of United Nations treaties are being conducted in the back of the minivan. My wife is a firm yet gentle mediator. When we disagree and a debate ensues, it usually goes badly for me. Maybe it's just me, but about halfway through an argument, I forget what my original point was. How does she do that? Such verbal sleight of hand! If truth be told, no man has ever really won an argument with his wife, the mother of his children. If you do win, you kind of lose in the long run. Our doghouse has room for only one dog, and it's a rough place to spend the night. I've kind of decided that she's too attractive to argue with, and that suits me just fine.

I think we can all agree that no one's *just a mom*. Mom is a big enough title for a gal to rock the world, and I got to see another example in the checkout line on a Thursday afternoon.

Glory Be Declaration

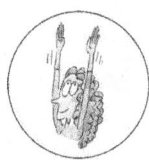

"Strength and honor are her clothing, and she can laugh at the time to come. Her mouth speaks wisdom, and loving instruction is on her tongue. She watches over the activities of her household and is never idle."

(Proverbs 31:25-31)

Matt Tullos

They DO Grow Up

My youngest son just called me. He passed the Armed Forces exams and is headed for the Army. I'm in a pool of happy, grateful tears right now. I've learned through time that they *do* grow up. Parenting is always a long series of detours, pit-stops, and roadblocks. And when you parent the *exceptionally different,* stuff just happens, especially on the odd years.

At three, he once got away from us. A manhunt ensued, and we found him in a boat in the middle of a pond, just laughing. Not a care in the world. Nobody else was laughing, but he was having the time of his life.

At four, he reveled with wonder at the fireworks show at the end of a long day at Disney. At the end of the show, hoisted on my shoulders, he shouted to everyone around, "Thank you for coming everyone!" I had no idea Caleb was a part owner.

At five, as a t-ball player, he'd hit the ball and run to tackle the infielder that caught it. He created his own sport. At first I was embarrassed, but then he won "most entertaining player," and I was proud. To this day we call it, "T-Rugby."

At seven, after the solemn Christmas Eve candlelight service, he picked up a huge twenty-candle candelabra fully lit and started singing, "Be Our Guest" from *Beauty and the Beast*. It was another harrowing deliverance from a possible disaster that could have required rescue personnel and fire trucks.

I'm not allowed to share anything more recent. The parental statute of limitations for embarrassing stories told on a son has not gone into effect. Despite the perilous years of doubt, dangers, disasters, and defeat, he has become a strong, courageous, radically devoted Christ-follower who has overcome Asperger's, dyslexia, bullying, and an often-failing father. He is my hero, and I couldn't be prouder.

And I won't tell any more stories, especially that one that involved the neighbor's cat, duct tape, and extra spicy salsa. That story will have to wait until later. Much, much later . . . .

Glory Be Declaration

"Sons are indeed a heritage from the Lord, offspring, a reward."

(Psalm 127:3)

My Mother Was a Cheapskate (Thank Goodness)

I'm so thankful for my mother. She made it to heaven this past year, but she left an indelible mark on my life. Growing up, I thought my mother was the strictest, most penny-pinching woman on the planet. As an adult, this theory has been confirmed. I used to think this was a flaw more than a virtue. I was wrong.

Mom was prepared for every crisis. The apocalypse, the tribulation, and the nuclear meltdown never happened, but if they did, the world would have turned to her and they would all receive stacks of canned hominy, frozen vegetables, and enough toilet paper to go around. But not the two-ply toilet paper. Much too expensive . . . .

I remember our weekly runs to the bread surplus store to get expired cinnamon bread at half price. If it weren't for the commercials, I wouldn't have even known that McDonald's served french fries until I was over the age of accountability. Birthday parties were senseless to her. I can still hear her say, "I'm so glad you were born, but after all those labor pains, I should be the one to get the presents." Yes, birthdays were celebrated, and gifts were given. I knew she was joking, but there was an imputed virtue in the middle of this humorous proverb—no one should get rewarded for just showing up on earth. We had to find our own jam and figure out how to play it well.

Along with her skill of saving, she mastered the art of discipline. She didn't have to lay a hand on me. Her laser-focused glare could singe my eyebrows from six hundred yards away. I used to complain that Mom made me go to bed earlier than any other child in North America. The only acceptable places to be after 8 p.m. were church or bed. Screen time wasn't an issue in our house. My big brother and I stayed out of the house for hours because we knew if we weren't studying, she'd have a list of activities on hand that involved brooms, scouring pads, and a variety of household cleaning chemicals. Of course, I was way too busy for this, so we usually braved the elements and rode our bikes like we were training for the Tour De France.

One of the greatest things my mom did growing up was force me to fail. She didn't just want me to feel the thrill of victory. She knew that I had to learn the agony of defeat. I still remember the day she yanked the training wheels off the bike without telling me. If she saw a fear or weakness in my psyche, she would push me in that direction. This kept me from the sin of cockiness. She knew that I had no sense of direction—none *whatsoever*—so she'd send me on errands that would surely get me lost in the streets of our small town. With no hand-eye coordination, she signed me up for piano lessons, which I enjoyed about as much as I did cleaning the grout . . . both of which were daily activities.

I can't play anything today, but it gave me the chutzpa to run toward the things I really enjoyed doing with an even greater passion.

Mom isn't with us this year, but she programmed me for success in so many ways, and whenever I get too big for my britches, I still feel her influence over me. I still tithe at church, watch my language, eat my vegetables, try to do more than what's expected, and, yes, I still put the seat down on the toilet.

I guess you could say I was sheltered as a child, and I am so thankful for it. Everyone needs shelter, especially in the culture our kids are growing up in these days.

Aha Moment

"Her children rise up and call her blessed; her husband also praises her."

(Proverbs 31:28)

My Six Catchphrases of Fatherhood

I thought it was just me, but probably not. There's nothing that will get you off the *dad pedestal* faster than catching your kids doing impressions of you. Here are six catchphrases that usually come out during apropos moments and fond recollections.

1. The redundant reprimand.
You're riding shotgun with your sixteen-year-old driving, and you believe that if you repeat something with escalating volume and rate it will somehow activate the brakes on the car: "Whoa . . . whoa . . . WHOA! WHOA!" It works. *Sometimes.* Other times . . . not so much. One thing's for sure: years later, when you are driving the family around, you're going to hear a family member shamelessly imitating you. They will remember the times you taught them to merge onto the highway: "Go . . . go . . . GO! GO!" They'll fondly recall your shotgun-seat command during breaking: "Stop . . . stop, stop, stop, STOP!" They'll give you a taste of your own medicine.

2. Krachamigen!
(Kra-cha-mi-gen)—said loudly *once*. It's kind of a German word. I don't know where it came from, but it just fell out of my mouth when I broke a water pipe at the house, which caused a water event akin to Old Faithful. Unfortunately for me, the entire family was there to witness the incident and to hear this verbal crouton in a bewildering word salad. I didn't cuss, but there was this word: *Krachamigen*! Ever since that day, the word has become a part of the family lexicon. Every occasion in which I seem to be losing my mind, a son will yell out, "Krachamigen!"

3. Who cares?
Men, never say this after a comment from your wife. Obviously, no matter how weird or insignificant the issue may seem to you, there is one person who does care: your wife. Proceed directly to the dog house. Do not pass go. Do not collect two hundred dollars.

4. Happy to entertain you.
One night after a long day, I fell asleep on the couch. I began a conversation with the family. But this conversation was different. I was talking in my sleep. Evidently this went on for several minutes and included topics such as llamas, pole vaulting, cruise ships, and marshmallows. By the time I woke up, I saw the whole family huddled around me as if I was a part of a hilarious interrogation. It was the most entertainment they'd enjoyed in weeks, and when I finally came back into consciousness, they were all laughing hysterically. That's when I said those famous words: "Happy to entertain you," as I stumbled to

the bedroom. Whenever I am the cause of unintentional laughter, someone in the family will repeat the phrase with a groggy tone of voice: "Happy to entertain you."

5. *He'd never do that!*

Arthur, our hairy golden retriever, loves this phrase. He understands it as well as, "Heel," "Sit," and "Stay." If someone in the family has a concern that Arthur might knock something over, eat the cake on the counter, or chase a squirrel into the house during spring cleaning, my response early on would be, "He'd never do that." This above-average dog eavesdrops and finds a way to do "that."

6. *How about later?*

I always seem to regret this one because *later* often means *never*, especially in those small, insignificant, once-in-a-lifetime moments like Lego™ building, kick-the-can, and those rare small talks with a teenage son. "How about later?" often means, "Not gonna happen"—because that's just the way life is. When you see a moment, even a little one, you'd better grab it. You might miss something amazing. Especially if it's overtime in the big game, the kids are gone, and your wife is feeling amorous. "How about later?" is just not a good response. Wait a second. I don't think I've ever said, "How about later?" to that.

Oh-No Admonition

"A human is like a breath; his days are like a passing shadow."

(Psalm 144:5)

October 31st Is Not My Favorite Day

It's the strangest, most awkward day of the year—Halloween. It's the one weird night out of the year where people celebrate the bad guys. I'll say up front, I don't like the idea of kids getting dressed up and scaring people. My kids do that just about every day of the year, so why rub it in?

I tend to be an excitable dad. My mind naturally goes to worst case scenarios. It's a character flaw that I've been working on for years. I'd like to say my first prayer when they handed my amazing first-born son was, *Lord, let this young man live long and prosper in the admonition of the Lord.* But alas, it was, *Lord Jesus, Son of God, do* not *let me drop him!* I'm not proud of it. I'm just being honest. My second prayer was, *Please let this shriveled-up thingy fall off his belly button correctly.*

Fear is not a spiritual gift, but if it was, I could lead seminars on it. I've got fear down pat. I've taken the tests. It's been confirmed by several mentors, family members, and three clinical psychologists. And if you watch the twenty-four-hour news cycle, you'll soon be on the fear bus that I've been on since I saw my first bigfoot documentary in the third grade. We're losing the ozone, the destruction of the rain forests. Every researcher finds a new habit, food, or lifestyle choice that causes cancer. Take artificial sweeteners, for example. If you use them, it supposedly changes your metabolism, and particles get caught inside your brain that take five years or so to flush out. If you don't use artificial sweeteners, you've got obesity and too many carbs. And have you noticed that no drinking water seems safe to anyone? We have bottled water now, but the plastic bottles have bisphenol and dioxins, which are "unhealthy." And tap? You're practically taking your life in your own hands, water boy.

Then take the issue of family. I could talk about that for hours. Hormones! Friends with tattoos and body piercings! Dating! Boyfriends! Girlfriends! Dubstep! Driving permits! Marriage conferences where you have knee-to-knee conversations with your wife for fifteen minutes at a time about your childhood wounds!

I haven't mentioned all the other things we need to fear: gum disease, retirement, warts, democrats, republicans, #metoo, tax reform, school lunches, artery health, gun control, hedge funds, depression that just jumps out at you from nowhere, Facebook viruses, fake news, terrorism, planes, trains, automobiles, the ring around the toilet, the ring around the collar, Russian moles, Twitter wars, Snapchat, Joy Behar, and sinkholes!

Who needs Halloween? There's plenty of stuff I can wrap my fearful mind around. But there's a formula I'm learning in all my years of phobic living. It's simple, and you know it too. *God is love. And His love casts out all fear.*

Life is full of tricks. But there is an amazing treat. And it's not in the form of a half-melted, fun-sized candy bar. It's in the glorious love of the fear-killing Redeemer who has everything under control.

Glory Be Declaration

"Do not fear, for I am with you; do not be afraid, for I am your God. I will strengthen you; I will help you; I will hold on to you with my righteous right hand."

(Isaiah 41:10)

Oh-No, Aha, and Glory Be

Matt Tullos

Two Steps Forward, One Step Back

Being a parent is the perfect metaphor of "two steps forward, one step back." It's just the way things work in parenting. I thought about that as my youngest son wheeled out of the drive in his '99 Subaru, loaded to the gills with his belongings to venture from the nest and into the great unknown. Parenting is uphill both ways. It's not a race to the finish line. There is no finish line, and many days it's a slow slog.

It's like those moments when you get your kitchen so clean that you could be considered *obsessive compulsive*, and then you walk into a family room flooded with the chaos of matchbox cars, action figures, building blocks, and dinosaurs (some of them slathered with chocolate pudding cups). Two steps forward, one step back.

I don't know how many times I've had to jump through all the hoops of getting the guys to bed, but now that we're past that stage, I've realized that hoop jumping was my superpower. A certain number of pages must be read, teeth need to be brushed, prayers must be said, and covers need to be adjusted. And just at the right time, they'd crave water like a Labrador Retriever in the Sahara Desert. It seemed like my boys were never tired until they collapsed. Darlene and I said what all parents say from time to time: "It's not about how tired you are, it's about how tired you are making us." After our last son, we relaxed as parents. We were so busy with the schedules of Upward Basketball, birthdays, carpools, parties, and science projects that we'd find him sprawled out on the family room floor with a half-eaten fruit roll-up in his little hand. Two steps forward, one step back.

We've missed a lot of adventures because we had kids. We've never been to those luxury resorts with crystal blue waters and not a stroller in a hundred miles. But we've been to a few amusement parks and wrestled a wild, squirming five-year-old for thirty minutes to administer amoxicillin. We found these moments both traumatizing and, I must confess, somewhat exciting. Sometimes they got so dirty the bathtub was out of the question. They were *backyard, spray-them-down-with-the-water-hose* dirty. We found parenting a rewarding rollercoaster ride of sound and fury, signifying a whole lot of stuff. Two steps forward, one step back.

I'm not a perfect parent, and we didn't raise perfect kids. Becoming a good father has been two steps forward and one step back. I said, "Maybe" when I was really thinking, *Yeah, that's not gonna happen.* For years I've stolen peanut butter cups from my sons on November 1st. I've made stuff up when the answers to their questions would require more wisdom and intelligence than I have at 5:30 in the morning. But now that they are gone, we still hear their voices echoing quietly through the house in our memories. They robbed our peace but stole our hearts. And that's for good. We treasure the days they return as adults for holidays and celebrations. Our role as parents has changed. We made progress even though it was two steps forward and one step back.

Aha Moment

"Brothers and sisters, I do not consider myself to have taken hold of it. But one thing I do: Forgetting what is behind and reaching forward to what is ahead, I pursue as my goal the prize promised by God's heavenly call in Christ Jesus."

(Philippians 3:13)

Matt Tullos

The Emoji Code of Parenthood

Shigetaka Kurita invented emojis in 1998. And you can tell from his name that he probably wasn't from Florence, Alabama. I'm somewhat of an emoji novice, but I'm catching up. It seems like emojis are advancing daily. You can say just about anything with emojis. Most teens I know are lightyears ahead of me in the vast subtleties of these little faces and objects. If you don't understand the linguistics of emojis, then you're probably having a difficult time texting with your teenage daughter.

In fact, I've seen some streams of texts that contain a long line of emojis that go back and forth between parties with no words. I guess the proverb is true: *Emojis fitly texted are like apples of gold.* (I think that's how it goes in the Message Bible.) These kinds of messages, for adults like me, require a millennial cryptologist to decipher. But I'm slowly learning the emoji code.

We all understand the simple smiley face emoji, but now we have the laughing with tears emoji. This rarely happens to me. I don't usually laugh with tears rolling down my face unless it's at the end of a youth lock-in or during allergy season, but it's rather popular with the young folks these days.

There's the upside-down smile emoji. It denotes silliness or sarcasm. This makes sense, but I can't remember ever standing on my head when I chose to be silly or sarcastic. Apparently, sarcasm is best delivered by gymnasts.

The half-smile rolling eyes emoji is a favorite among my sons, especially when I try to text a joke, offer condescending advice, challenge their political views, or make a comment on a selfie, or any time that I happen to be texting. When I see it, I reply with the *nerdy-smiling-guy-with-glasses* emoji.

If you'd ask me about my favorite emoji, I'd have to say it's the taco emoji. Not because I am that much of a connoisseur of Tex-Mex or fast food. There's a little story that goes with it. A couple of years ago my sixteen-year-old said to me, "I'm glad that you love me, but this texting 'I love you' is a little cumbersome and annoying. Let's just use a taco to say it. It's so much easier and less embarrassing when I'm around my friends."

Nothing warms my heart more than to see the taco emoji on my phone at midnight from my university son who's 784 miles away. It's father/son code that God is amazing, being a dad is worth it all, and I've finally found the crypto-key to the parental emoji code.

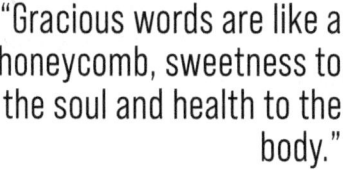

"Gracious words are like a honeycomb, sweetness to the soul and health to the body."
(Proverbs 16:24)

Reflections on Launching

I remember the day Nathan went to college. He was only a few hours away, but it seemed like a much farther distance than that. In truth, it was. He would come home to visit for a day or two, but as most young, romantic sons with heads full of dreams, he has found his wings. He was a middle son, so many times he'd be caught in the vortex of life in our home. It's easy for middle sons to get lost in the background. He is such a great guy. I hope you'll get to meet him some day.

Recently after graduating from Lee University, his lust for adventure led him to Chicago. He's 913.2 miles away from where we live in Louisiana. He's out on his own, making a career, loving life, and learning about God. I'm proud, but I must say, I regret that I didn't more fully appreciate the moments we had. As Don Herold said it best, "We had our moments. But I wish we would have had more of them." We text three or four times a day now. He's learning about insurance, taxes, and fuel pumps, and he's looking for his girl. Although I've never met her and he hasn't either, I'm praying for her daily.

We have a tendency to get so lost in the muddled mess that we miss the true blessings of life that are right there in front of us, and we don't celebrate them. I've often been guilty of that. I remember a haunting line I read years ago: "We shout at our kids, 'Why don't you grow up.' But one day the walls of our empty rooms will echo back, 'We did.'"

I don't know where you are in this journey of parenthood, but today is sacred. In fact, the very best moment in life is today. Today is a gift that is moving forward faster than thoughts or plans. Today is where I am right here and right now. Today is an opportunity to change the little things.

Today is closer. Tomorrow is not a promise, and yesterday is an eternity from anything I could attain. Today is most noble. Today is most daring.

Tomorrow hopes, but today is. God holds the future and redeems all of yesterday, but today is closer, and today is where I find God.

I hope when you read this you will be grateful for this moment. I hope that you are grateful for where you are and what an amazing concept today, right now, really is. I hope that today you aren't planning a siege on your enemy. I hope you aren't wasting this moment trying to prove that you are right. I hope you aren't swallowed up in regret. I hope that if you have kids, they're getting the very best hours of your day. I hope you aren't poisoning your time with trivial, toxic thoughts of wealth, vanity, or revenge. None of that really works anyway. Does it?

I hope you are in the moment because this moment is sculpting your destiny. You live; therefore, you are here *today*!

Oh-No Admonition

"Yet you do not know what tomorrow will bring—what your life will be! For you are like vapor that appears for a little while, then vanishes."

(James 4:14)

Oh-No, Aha, and Glory Be

Shared Labor & Super Glue

School is in full swing, and I am already making late night runs to twenty-four-hour pharmacies and grocery stores for supplies to use in my kids' projects and presentations. Somewhere in the world I am sure that money is passing hands between a shadow representative of schools and the school supply vendors to ensure that glue sticks, project boards, permanent markers, and molding clay are in demand. Last night I went on a safari through the formidable chasms of the dreaded craft store to find something . . . anything that would serve as vegetation for my son's dinosaur diorama. I ran into another dad who had the same crazy shopping list I had.

I looked over at him and simply said, "Mrs. Stokes? Eighth grade science?"

He smiled and said with an empathetic chuckle, "You got it, man."

I'd never heard of a diorama until my first son hit third grade. Now I am the duke of dioramas, the prince of the projects. I know what type of glue adheres small rocks to a poster. I can smell a laminator a mile off. I can create a nontoxic volcano eruption that Spielberg would be proud for his grandson to display. One of my friends who has less time and scruples than I do told me he finished his son's project the same day as it was assigned. "No way! How'd you do that?" He winked at me and whispered, "Craig's List. An insect display complete with fifteen insect specimens from the same ecosystem for only seventy-five bucks." I thought to myself, *You are an evil, evil man.* There is an ethical man code that was broken that day, and he didn't even bat an eye.

For me, school projects are a mix of parent-child quality time with a dash of codependency. My parents didn't do nearly as much as I do for the students in my home. But then again, I am convinced that projects are being assigned so often that even NASA would struggle meeting deadlines on some syllabi.

So far this year I have—I mean, *we* have—created a coat of arms, a scaled replica of Stonehenge, a Native American meal and a short greeting in their tribal language, a Revolutionary War timeline, and a collection of original haikus (which my son had to do over because I got haikus and limericks mixed up. And yes, I'm embarrassed. I do know the difference. I was just really busy trying to fix our leaky toilet when he asked, and I misremembered.).

School projects are also a metaphor for parenting. We are scrambling to keep up, learning things we didn't learn from our parents, and trying to help our kids without creating too big of a mess. We send them off into the world with memories of shared labor and superglue.

The practicality of these projects may be in question, but one thing is sure: if I ever accidentally enter a time machine and end up in the ancient world of the Navaho, I'll know exactly what they are eating and how to say hello.

Aha Moment

"The slacker craves, yet has nothing, but the diligent is fully satisfied."
(Proverbs 13:4)

Upgrading the Antennae

My son is a church planter on a gaming platform as I write this, and yet I don't even know what it means. Not exactly. Evidently he's built a church on a game map, and then he invites gamers to come to the Bible study in the gaming universe. All the members keep their game weapons outside the edifice Caleb somehow constructed in the "Earth 2" universe. As a side note, I don't think I've ever had to remind church members in the real world, *Hey, church, we've got a business meeting this Wednesday night. Be sure to drop your heavy ammo, nuclear weapons, bananas, trip wires, rocket launchers, and power packs in the vestibule.*

I overheard a little bit of a meeting. (Please don't tell him I was snooping. Let's keep that between you and me.) It was amazing. I'd never seen him lead out in anything. He's quiet at church. He fades into the background. But with an Xbox live account and a Message Bible, he's a twenty-first-century church starter in the making.

What I've come to understand is that Caleb is on a different frequency, and if I want to connect with him, I need a bigger antennae. Period. Each of my four sons transmits things in a way that is uniquely theirs. Darlene does too. There is not a family cookie cutter. Every family member is different. Although it's a no brainer, I never really understood that until we had two kids. When Jacob was born, the first thing I said as I held him those first few moments of his life was, "He's different!" Subconsciously I suppose I just thought I'd have another Isaac—but no! He even had a different smell. Not bad, just different. When Jacob was born, I realized that I immediately had to upgrade my antennae.

Many times my antennae isn't up! Don't you just hate when the people you love most are telling you something, and the last sentence ends with a question, and you realize that she's waiting for an answer and you weren't even listening to the question? And we all struggle with listening. The best listener in our family is Arthur. Arthur never interrupts. He accepts whatever you say. He's un-shockable. He provides positive feedback, and he never, *ever* judges. I started asking myself, *What makes Arthur different from everyone else in the family?* And then it came to me: he's our golden retriever. In truth, Arthur has really saved me a lot of money on counseling.

As humans though, we all have reception issues. We learn differently. As Gary Chapman has taught for over forty years, we love differently, and we worship differently. We all do life differently. We were designed differently. These differences have the ability to make us an amazing family and to drive us absolutely, stark-raving bananas. I'll never stop trying to upgrade my antennae, but a Bible study with people who have rocket launchers still gives me the willies.

Oh-No Admonition

"He said, 'If you listen carefully to the Lord your God and do what is right in his eyes, if you pay attention to his commands and keep all his decrees, I will not bring on you any of the diseases I brought on the Egyptians, for I am the Lord, who heals you.'"

(Exodus 15:26)

They Really Do Say the Darndest Things

Observing my sons expanding their vocabulary often led to a cavalcade of baffling, serendipitous moments in parenting. Yogi Berra had nothing on my boys.

After Isaac was born, our doctor encouraged us to just calendar the date for the birth of his brothers. Pitocin (that drug that gets the process going) would make sure of that. Isaac had overheard too much and managed to get the semantics a little backwards when he told the pastor, "Mom will be seduced on Friday." I peppered in the correction quickly, "Induced! Induced!" Pastor Joe just laughed and whispered to me, "Looks to me like that's already happened."

We worked hard to create opportunities to teach the Bible to our kids. With boys enhanced with a little too much high-fructose corn syrup, this time was like the floor of the Merck Exchange during a pork belly sell-off. Unnecessary comments, baffling questions, and malodorous fumes often sent me retreating from the room and wondering if this was really what Moses had in mind when he wrote Deuteronomy 6. During one of our many trips to the grandparents, our seven-year-old, Jacob, asked, "Daddy, since we're here, do we still have to do demotionals?"

After Easter, several kids were talking about their church experience the day before. One stated that they sang songs about Jesus. Another said they drew pictures of Jesus. Caleb, not to be outdone, chose to recall our dramatic presentation by telling the other kids, "Well, we crucified Him at our church." I wasn't around to restate the facts to the other kids who might have been traumatized by the activities of our church, but thankfully the kindergarten teacher was.

The development of the brain in all human boys causes many fathers to scratch their heads. Multisyllabic words and complex art forms are ahead, and they'll even know what they are and how to use them in due time. But the most important words that I still want them to remember are the one-syllable ones: *God, love, grace, truth, hope, joy,* and (of course) *home*. These are big words. Simple but also complicated at times. They are the ones that count.

Oh-No Admonition

"Repeat them to your children. Talk about them when you sit in your house and when you walk along the road, when you lie down and when you get up."

(Deuteronomy 6:6)

Matt Tullos

Parental Superpowers

My mom had superpowers. Lots of them. Nothing seemed to get past her. She somehow knew that I secretly raided the cupboard for condensed milk during household candy shortages. She had five cans. I just took one! Who counts cans for crying out loud? Answer: My mom didn't have to. She had superpowers, and she saved that slice of counterintelligence about the Eagle Brand disappearance for the optimum moment of dramatic revelation.

She could, with laser precision, spot me from fifty feet away where she was seated in the back of the choir loft. It may have been a note I was passing to a friend nearby, a paper airplane I constructed from the church bulletin, marbles I would roll down the slanted auditorium aisle, or the small transistor radio that I stealthily slipped into my ear during the offertory prayer—she saw it all. Make no mistake, I wouldn't even be looking in her direction. Suddenly a warm sensation would wash over me. The sensation would grow warmer, and I'd feel sick. *What is this?* I'd ask myself. And then I glanced toward the platform. It was my mother's piercing glare.

Dad was a manly man who could and did fight bobcats and pit bulls in the hills of north Louisiana. Still, I didn't fear my father. My mother was the one that had superpowers.

With the X-ray vision of Superman, the grip of Spiderman, the righteous indignation of The Incredible Hulk, the grace of Wonder Woman, and a black Chrysler New Yorker that ironically looked a lot like the Batmobile, this action-hero mom stood as victor in every single episode against me, the Joker.

I wish I inherited some of that superpower swag my mom had. She had superswag before the word *swag* was invented. Not swag, in the hip-hop sense. This was parental swag. It's the swagger of a parent who always held her ground no matter what sudden challenge her four offspring would throw her way.

I've rarely had X-ray vision to see the antics of my sons. Most days I am oblivious. I've walked through every stage of parenting with great fear and trepidation. Conversely, my mom, who grew up just after the Great Depression, learned from her parents that weeding flower beds, not getting a weekly allowance, and not having the latest and greatest toy or gadget, would not kill the child but in truth would make him stronger.

Mom taught me a phrase that solves many problems and that I don't think I've used enough. This five-word response covers a multitude of missteps: "I love you, but no."

"I love you, but no" allows every child the opportunity later in life to thwart even the most dastardly villains and immensely impossible predicaments.

Aha Moment

"She watches over the activities of her household and is never idle."

(Proverbs 31:27)

Oh-no, Aha, and Glory Be

Matt Tullos

I've Lost It!

One of my favorite things these days is the Bluetooth key finder. I don't know how I've survived all these years without the aid of this deft invention. I don't just have one. I have six! One for my keys, my brief case, my security badge, my journal, my wallet, and my Bible. I travel to lots of churches, and I've become somewhat of an accidental Gideon, leaving Bibles in hotel rooms, Sunday school classes, and even bathrooms. Personally, I can only focus on one thing at a time. It's a disability, but it doesn't make me eligible for the special parking spaces. When I am focused on a conversation, a task, or a problem, everything else fades to black. I've spent approximately two and a half years combined scurrying through homes, offices, and airport terminals looking for things. Now there's an app for that, and I spend more time actually living life and less time searching for those things I've got to have.

There are lots of lost things in the Bible. There's the lost coin, the lost son, the lost ark, the lost glory, and even the lost young Messiah. Joseph and Mary somehow lost Jesus on their way back from the temple. I think *that* story is my favorite one for a couple of reasons. First, it reminds me that sometimes I forget to bring Jesus with me when I leave church on Sunday. I've got to take Him with me or else I'll spend the next few days with the strange notion that something is discombobulated inside. Another reason I like that story so much is that our family once left one of our kids in the nursery after church. We were in separate cars. Imagine the shock of that arrival home. "I thought you were getting him!"—Darlene and I said simultaneously as we hopped in the car and raced back to the church. I've never been one for inserting a tracking chip on your child for exact location coordinates, but don't think I haven't pondered the possibility.

You know what the greatest thing about losing stuff is? It's that moment when they are found. The elation when you realized that the keys were stuffed between the couch cushions, or the Bible was left at the Welcome Center at church, or the sudden euphoria when some kind soul finds your wallet at the coffee shop and lays it at your front door with a note and all the cards and bills intact. To me, there's nothing better. Maybe it's so great because it reminds me of the joy of the Father when lost sons and daughters return home.

Aha Moment

"For the Son of Man has come to seek and to save the lost."

(Luke 19:10)

Kids and Permanent Markers (Not a Good Idea)

How have we hidden them? On top of the refrigerator, in the top drawer of a dresser, or guarded by Navy Seals in an iron safe and monitored by infrared security alarms. *Somehow* my kids would find a way to get them and use them.

We moved into our dream home a few years back. We were all so delighted with all the extra space. It was really the first home Darlene had been able to plan everything from the paint to the carpet to the kitchen island. She was in heaven. We watched expectantly as the last brick was in place and the last roll of carpet had been installed.

As we joyously walked into the home that first morning, I said to my youngest son who had just turned three, "This house is so big, you might not be able to find you room!" I should have been more discerning as I looked at his worried little face as he pursed his little lips together and furrowed his brow at that one comment.

I knew something was wrong when I awoke the next morning to the sound of my wife's plaintive wail. I rushed out of the bedroom and immediately understood her sorrow. Our youngest had taken a magic marker and drawn a line from the front door down the foyer, up the stairs, into his room . . . ending the line with the point of an arrow fixed in place at the foot of his bed. He explained, as best he could, that he didn't want to forget where his room was. A thick, red, felt-tip pen on eggshell carpet does not help the resale value, but it does remind us to pray for our children.

We've had a number of similar incidents. Since we wouldn't let our kids do the temporary tattoos from the cereal boxes—in an attempt to teach Levitical law to them (see Leviticus 19:23-28)—they took turns creating eagles or some other type of winged creatures on each other's bellies. Suffice it to say, they found a work-around. At least it wasn't on their foreheads.

They found many other applications and surfaces for permanent markers:

- On the couch to reserve a permanent seat
- On the wall to record important milestones
- On the cat paws (why? why not?)

- On rags (hurriedly cleaning up the marker stains before they got busted)
- On the pages of my *Thompson's Chain Reference Bible*. (One son thought the black and white outlined maps were coloring pages. I actually saw this happen to my Study Bible while I was preaching with my large print Bible. What a helpless feeling. It's impossible to interject, "Jacob, stop that," in the middle of a message about the eternity of our souls.)

My greatest prayer these days is that when my children are old, God will make a much more permanent mark on their souls. Every stroke of parenting, every opportunity to bless and discipline leaves a spiritual and emotional mark. Daily I'm reminded of the things we did and the things that we didn't do to aid them on their journey. We made our mark, but if I had it to do all over again, I'd make more of them.

One thing is for certain: I'm an expert on permanent marker removal, and if you need help, hunt me down on Facebook. I'll walk you through it.

"Bind them as a sign on your hand and let them be a symbol on your forehead."
(Deuteronomy 6:8)

4 Days in November

Darlene is planning to leave this week for a class reunion, and this time I'm ready. Previous experiences and incidents demand readiness on my part. I remember all the things I've learned in the past, and hopefully they'll prepare me for the next four days. Luckily my kids are all out of diapers and no longer require certain types of hypoallergenic food products. As I reflect on those years of fatherhood, I have to smile at all the panicked moments and last minute saves. I have a much deeper appreciation for the trials of a single mom. Hats off to you, ladies.

I'd call the process *parental entropy*. *Entropy* is defined as the process of the natural world in which the environment moves from order to disorder in isolated systems. Without my wife, I am the poster child for "isolated systems." Allow me to illustrate the concept:

Day one: Everything is great. The first couple of hours would receive the Focus on the Family Seal of Approval. The TV is off, the kids are playing politely in the living room with Bible hero action figures, and carrot sticks are available for optional consumption. By bedtime, the rooms aren't too messy, and the kids were so good I let them stay up an extra hour.

Day two: I begin to feel a little out of control but still ahead of the game. I'm just a little confused by how empty pudding cups could be affixed to the kitchen wall and why the cat has duct tape wrapped around his torso. I call an inquisition, but what is a parent to do when your boys each point to each other as catalysts of the chaos?

Day three: I haven't shaved since she left. I feel like I'm bringing up the rear in the Olympics of single parenthood. I finally get around to looking on the list Darlene has left me about things that have to happen, and I realize that I am to be the provider of paper plates and cupcakes for my third grader's class party. (This was long before cupcake franchises were conceived.) For some reason, I was cited in a school zone for hitting a curb and going the wrong way in the drop-off line. I tried explaining that I was distracted by the salamander my oldest son had slipped in my shirt. Simply because I couldn't produce the creature, it was not considered a credible explanation!

Day four: Her arrival being only three hours away, I skip work and call three senior adult widows from my church who help me return the house to its normal state. Darlene arrived to find her home only slightly disheveled and was mildly surprised that I was able to do so well without her.

When Darlene reads this, I hope I can claim the six-year statute of marital limitations.

After a handful of these experiences, I am reminded how blessed I am to have a multitasking bride. I am convinced that Proverbs 31, the ode of a virtuous woman, was written twenty-five-hundred years ago after the author's wife had left for a week-long women's conference in Jericho. In my home, it really takes three to parent: a dad, a mom, and the Messiah. And, I might add, not in that order. More than any other lesson, being a dad reminds me that I am not equipped to go it alone. I must have the help of a wife, a church, a gracious God, lots of deodorizing products, hard candy, and microwavable kids' meals.

Glory Be Declaration

"Her mouth speaks wisdom, and loving instruction is on her tongue. She watches over the activities of her household and is never idle."

(Proverbs 31:26-27)

And My Diagnosis Is . . .

Our society emerged as an over-diagnosed culture over the past ten years. We seem to have a name for just about every disease, dysfunction, and disorder. I don't know why, but I guess it's a good thing to be able to understand ourselves or at least have an excuse for the crazy things we do! Through twenty-four years of being a dad, I thought I'd hop on the bandwagon. Perhaps you have experienced one or two of these:

- *Dejavuphobia:* A sudden fear that my son will make the same embarrassing mistakes on his first date that I made on mine.
- *O-snap-athy:* Waking up in a panic on Saturday morning, thinking that everyone in the house overslept for school.
- *Sockfunkify:* The strange odor emanating from your kid's bedroom after soccer practice.
- *Hyper-fossilicity:* The ability of old, stray french fries to become rock hard in your car after two weeks.
- *Exchangopathy:* Car key confusion when car keys are exchanged back and forth from my key ring and my son's key ring.
- *Minivanusitis:* A short-term curvature of the spine after a sixteen-hour drive to the grandparents' home.
- *Explodeanese:* The unintelligible language that bursts forth when teaching a child how to drive.
- *Involuntary Streakification:* Running out of the shower when you hear blood-curdling screams from your three-year-old.
- *Actorision:* The insincere apology of a twelve-year-old who used your formal dining plates to attempt a juggling feat as seen on *America's Got Talent*.
- *Photographic Fingernitis:* The cramp in your pointer finger after videoing a thirty-minute school play.
- *Chucky Cheesoring:* Attempts to eliminate the ringing in your ear after three hours at your five-year-old's birthday party.

And then there's my favorite:

- *Blessuphoria:* Accidentally catching your daughter reading her Bible before heading off to school.

May you have more blessuphoria than involuntary streakifications!

Aha Moment

"The end of a matter is better than its beginning; a patient spirit is better than a proud spirit."
(Ecclesiastes 7:8)

Matt Tullos

Dadsplaining No More

Early in the twenty-first century, a term arose from popular culture: *mansplaining*. It's when a man will over-explain things to a female. It's kind of like a husband explaining the eccentricities of a cover-two defense to his wife whose father is a defensive coordinator for the Patriots. Or a man explaining spiritual strongholds to Beth Moore.

But there is a deeper, more common version of mansplaining: *dadsplaining*. This is the dad that over-explains things to his kids. I come from a long line of dadsplainers. When I would come home from college, my dad used to love taking me to the movies. He preferred taking me to movies that he had already seen. About every two minutes during the movie, he would whisper a running commentary about what was going on. For example, as the undercover detective was rummaging through the garbage of a Russian spy, my dad would lean over to me and say, "See . . . he's looking for evidence that Nikita works for the Kremlin. And he's about to find out that it's Nikita's wife that's the real spy!" I wanted to buy him a t-shirt with an arrow pointing to his head with the words "Spoiler Alert" screen printed on it.

But I must confess that the dadsplaining gene has been passed to me. It doesn't show up around work associates or my wife (I know better), but something in me wants to explain to my kids things that they probably have a better understanding of than I do. I can tell it's happening because their eyes involuntarily begin to roll. That's my cue to stop talking and start asking them questions because I'm probably articulating a little more than I know.

Most dads feel behooved to know the answers to all of life's mysteries, such as how to program a universal remote or the correct way to clip a dog's toenails. But I am slowly learning to listen more to my kids as they enter adulthood. None of my guys like the word *should*. Honestly, I don't either.

It was so much easier to dadsplain when my sons were trying to learn how to ride a bike or negotiate rush-hour traffic at age fifteen. It's more difficult as they navigate their careers—one in music, one in a startup company, one laying siege to Calculus 3, and one heading in uniform to some unnamed location in Afghanistan. These are the lives of my kids, and I pray one hundred times more than I dadsplain. You see, I know little about musical theory. I'm tone deaf. I am clueless to instill correct business acumen. I wasn't even aware that there was a Calculus 3 up until three days ago, and I couldn't pass it if my life depended on it. And I have no idea how my army son got the strength and bravery to be deployed. I can't explain any of that. I find that being a compassionate and present listener yields far more benefits to those I love than dadsplaining. I must look heavenward with thanksgiving, admiration, and mystery. One day God will do the explaining.

Oh-No Admonition

"When arrogance comes, disgrace follows, but with humility comes wisdom."

(Proverbs 11:2)

Family Overboard

Last spring, Darlene thought it would be great for us to take our sons and their girlfriends whitewater rafting. She went whitewater rafting in Colorado on a mission trip during high school, but that was back when Amy Grant was just getting popular. In the voice of a thousand memes, she said, "This will be fun!" Sure it will! Darlene signed us up online. She paid careful attention to the various prices for each journey. Being a smart shopper, she booked us for the least expensive journey available down the Ocoee River. During our orientation before the adventure began, we discovered that we were slated to raft down the Olympic course. This most challenging leg of the journey had been created for the 1996 Olympics in Atlanta. What? As time passed, I felt compelled to memorialize the experience. First, they detailed every possible fatality that could be experienced on an inflatable raft. Every cautionary scenario was covered, apart from being attacked by a marauding bear. We were told to float on our backs if we capsized. "Don't fight the water. Just go limp." They showed us all the rescue techniques, but they were talking so fast I just couldn't process all the information. We all looked at each other with cautionary glances and raised eyebrows. "Let's do this!" one of our boys shouted. Our tour guide, Caden, was eighteen and had only escorted one other group down this stretch of river. We were too far in to bail at this point, but we all saw our lives flash before our eyes.

They've got nicknames for different parts of the river, and when we got to "tombstone rapids," the next thing I remember is the boat flipping, catapulting me completely airborne. Then I found myself *under* the boat, with one shoe missing and my helmet on backwards. I don't have any idea how it happened. It was like the twister scene in *The Wizard of Oz*, but instead of the old lady in the rocking chair and the flying cow, the sons and the girlfriends swirled around me like puppies learning to dogpaddle. There was no "going limp" for me! I had no idea where the wife was! Kansas, maybe? Suddenly, I was plucked out of the water and onto a boat of Chinese tourists who didn't speak a lick of English. It felt like the Olympics course for a totally different reason. I scanned the shore for Darlene. When I finally spotted her, she was about fifty yards away, sitting on a boulder in the middle of the river. How did that happen? She didn't even know. We got back on the raft we started on, but the rest of the trip I kept thinking about all the ways we could have died. For a moment, I imagined meeting Jesus at the threshold of heaven with a surprised look on His face, saying, *What are you doing here? You went rafting!* I know that's not how it would go down, but that was my divine vision. Darlene came away with a black eye, which made going out in public a little precarious for me. We felt obligated to tell the story to strangers over and over and over for the next couple of weeks.

Yes, certain experiences in life are metaphors. And this time the lessons were pretty simple: When life gets turned upside down, relax and trust that your family or even strangers will pull you back to safety. The best way to stay in the boat is to keep rowing. And be prepared for the rapids. They're just a part of the journey.

When it warms up again, we will just go tubing.

Oh-No Admonition

"Trust in the Lord with all your heart, and do not rely on your own understanding; in all your ways know him, and he will make your paths straight."

(Proverbs 3:5-6)

Oh-No, Aha, and Glory Be

Fond Moments of Clarity

As dads, we have the unique opportunity to reveal truth to our children. We get the chance to tell them how life works. These conversations happen along the way. They are unforgettable, sometimes unpredictable, and other times just plain weird. Here's one example:

The context: While driving down the interstate, having just listened on CD to Dr. James Dobson explain the mechanics of sex.
Son: So that's what you and Mom did when you had us?
Me: Yes.
Son: So you did that four times?
Me: Well, at least.
Son: You mean you and Mom have done that more than four times?
Me: Yes.
Son: In our house?
Me: Yes. Yes, we did. But we've done it on vacations too.
Son: REALLY?
Me: Let me think. Well, yes.
Son: But not at Disney World. Please don't tell me you did that at Disney World.
Me: Actually . . . let's see . . . [I'm beginning to get nervous in the presence of my ten-year-old. The father-son trip seemed to have taken on the feel of a congressional hearing] I mean . . . um . . . not at Magic Kingdom, for goodness' sake, but at the resort when you were . . . um . . . with your grandparents.
Son: I see you two kissing and hugging. But that? That is what you did?
Me: Yes. We did that.
Son: But not anymore, right?
Me: Actually we kind of do.
Son: Still?
My son's face becomes pale. His breathing labored.
Son: Dad, stop the car. I think I'm going to throw up.

This was a greater miscarriage of childhood than the truth about Santa and the baseball doping scandal. Perhaps it was a preemptive strike upon his naiveté, but the truth was there under the light of day. The toothpaste was out of the tube, and there was no turning back. His parents were having sex. Lots of sex.

Our son Nathan, now in college, still remembers that long drive into the dawn of manhood.

It was the first of many conversations we have had about the hijinks of monogamous marital bliss and other gritty subjects every father must unpack with a son. We've talked about lots of other strange and wonderfully embarrassing subjects, but I'll never forget the pit-stop on I-40 when my innocent son threw up after getting the low down on his parents and their scandalous activities that brought him into the world.

"You will know the truth, and the truth will set you free."

(John 8:32)

Oh-No, Aha, and Glory Be

Curfews and Cautionary Tales

Last night, I anxiously waited for my son to return from a party. This was one of the first times he would be going with a friend in a friend's car. The party was at the home of a church member I trusted, and my son had his phone, but honestly I was a little embarrassed by my parental gaffe. I couldn't remember if the curfew I set was 10 or 10:30. I'm sure we talked about it, but I really didn't want to get in a fuss about the details, especially if they weren't written down.

As I sat on the porch waiting for the sound of the 90s German jalopy that I saw him climb into earlier that last evening, I suddenly had insight into my nervousness. It took me back to 1979 when I went to my first homecoming dance. This was my first date. I was a good kid under the rule of strict parents, so I guess it slipped their minds to set up a curfew for me. They trusted me. Right? Surely I would use my brain and get home at a reasonable hour. This was my first school dance. I'd never danced before. I was a Baptist, for goodness sake. The music played on that night, and everybody else seemed to be fairly unconcerned about the time. I was just a guy with two left feet, trying everything I could to bust a move to a ten-minute-long version of a Bee Gees hit.

It must have been 1 a.m. when I rolled into the driveway of the Tullos home. I went in, locked the doors, and prepared for bed, still basking in the glow of my first date. About a minute later, I heard the doorbell ring. *Strange . . . who would be ringing our doorbell at one in the morning?* I went to the front door, and there was my dad. Angry. And in nothing but his underwear. Dad had seen the lights of the car rolling into the drive as he waited for my arrival. He went out the front door to confront me. He wasn't quick enough. By the time he walked around the lawn to the back of the house, I had already gone in and locked him out.

The lecture that night must have lasted an hour, and my days on the dance floor came to a swift conclusion.

So now it's my turn to sit at the window and wait for my son. That crazy night proved to be a cautionary tale about the importance of proper time management and communication. My son Caleb came home well before the clock struck 10, and all was once again well. Time controversies subsided. But the picture of my dad in his underwear at the front door is forever burned into my memory.

Aha Moment

"Therefore don't worry about tomorrow, because tomorrow will worry about itself. Each day has enough trouble of its own."

(Matthew 6:34)

Matt Tullos

March: Everyone Knows It's Windy

I don't know how March is in your corner of the universe, but in Tennessee, it's the month that can't make up its mind. I've lived in New Orleans when March is pretty consistent: eighty-three degrees, afternoon showers, and an occasional breeze that makes you wish for the fifties that you had during a couple of days in February. I lived in Amarillo, where the one consistency is the wind—a constant forty miles per hour year-round. In the winter, the snow doesn't hit the ground. It flies vertically, and what doesn't smack you in the face lands somewhere in western Oklahoma. Tennessee Marches have an identity crisis. March doesn't know what it wants to be from day to day.

The wind is a great metaphor of the human experience. Jesus said, "The wind blows where it pleases" (John 3:8). Meteorologists have been humbled by this truth. I have been too. When I was a part-time jailer during grad school, the wind locked me inside a paddy wagon when its gust slammed the doors shut. It wasn't my finest hour. The wind blew a term paper out of my backpack in high school long before I knew the value of a floppy disk. (Millennials: ask your parents what a floppy disk is.) The wind blew a couple of letters off our church sign. It went from "KNOW JESUS" to "NO JESUS." It blew up on Facebook before we could find the K and the W.

As parents, we can choose what kind of wind we are.

You can be a hurricane. When you see your kids panicked by your forecasted arrival, boarding their windows and scrounging for water bottles before evacuation, it's a good sign that you might want to increase your grace.

You can be a twister—a little less predictable than a hurricane but just as destructive. You touch down, and before your family knows it, there are cows, tractors, grandmas, and rocking chairs swirling above them. The barometric pressure of outbursts can be off the charts during those tornado days.

Instead, let's be the cool breeze that consistently powers the windmills of their spiritual growth. It makes the outside world a bit more manageable. You can't control the weather that life throws at you, but you can adjust the climate in your home. When you learn that skill, you'll be blown away with the results.

Oh-No Admonition

"Be angry and do not sin. Don't let the sun go down on your anger, and don't give the devil an opportunity."

(Ephesians 4:26)

Glory Days

In 2016 we moved from Tennessee to my hometown in Louisiana. This town in Central Louisiana is filled with memories. The other day I returned to the same barber shop that I frequented as a child. It was déjà vu all over again, as Yogi Berra once said. It's been great for my two younger sons to see the stomping grounds of their father, but I'm sure they've grown tired of all the yarns I've been spinning.

"That's where I went on my first date!"

"Hey! That's the field where I scored a touchdown in peewee football. Let's jump the fence, and I'll recreate the play!"

Caleb and Nathan look at each other with a tolerant expression that brought me back to reality.

"Maybe some other time," I said, knowing that I had reached my story limit. Until, that is, I took them along for a barbeque with a number of my long lost friends from college. When they started talking, Caleb and Nathan were all ears.

Suddenly they were enlightened. One story led to another, and my buddies completely ignored my subtle expressions and more obvious hand gestures as their razor-sharp memories kicked into gear.

"Guys, your dad was quite the exhibitionist in college. His freshman year, we dumped him out at the front of the campus on his birthday wearing only his BVDs."

"Boxers or the other kind?" Caleb asked inquisitively.

"The other kind, of course. I never knew how nimble and quick he could run. Dodging in and out of shrubs . . . between trees."

"And then there was the time he put alarm clocks all over the chapel and set them to go off at the very end because the speakers always went over time. That was epic. He and Eric, that missionary kid, put one in the piano, one up in the balcony, one under the platform chair, and one inside the pulpit. The dean of students and the president showed mercy, and it's a good thing. Your dad really doesn't have any marketable skills other than the ministry."

It was a nightmare! My sons yucking it up with middle-aged classmates.

The Holy Spirit whispered softly in King James, "Whatever a man soweth, that shall he also reapeth." I knew I was reapeth-ing twenty-seven-year-old "soweth."

My friend, who is now a doctor, chimed in. "Remember that girl that Matt dated that was so temperamental? Matt was head over heels in love with her, but he kept calling her by the name of his old girlfriend that dropped him the month before. That reeeally made her mad."

"I bet it did," Nathan chuckled, gleefully enjoying my jittery disposition.

I found an opening in the conversation and went for it. "So Dave, is your son still in town?"

"Nope. He's in Wasilla, Alaska. And then there was that time when we almost got arrested for bringing the cow statue on the mini trailer from the Sizzlin' Steakhouse into that English professor's office after we flunked a pop quiz he gave."

I couldn't knock them off course. I tried to dismiss the oft-corroborated testimony of my dear old friends, but the eyewitness testimony did me in. I am thankful that grace is the message of Christ. Our past is history, thank goodness. But God has a way of reminding us that we are all works in progress. We still are. The paint is still wet, and the cement hasn't dried. God sees me that way, and thanks to the tall tales of some longwinded friends, my family knows that my life was and still is a messy adventure.

Oh-No Admonition

"But if you don't do this, you will certainly sin against the Lord; be sure your sin will catch up with you."

(Numbers 32:23)

I Didn't See that Coming

Perhaps the most surprising thing about our journey as a family is that it is so surprising. The most predictable thing about life is its singular unpredictability. Think about all the things that you've experienced in your family that caused you to shake your head and say, "Well, I didn't see that coming."

I'd venture to say that most of us grew up watching TV dramas where the dog was lost and then found, or the misunderstanding was neatly clarified, or the seemingly impossible rescue was attained in fifty-nine minutes with room for ten minutes of commercials. But then we encounter the glorious, sometimes maddening concept of *real life*.

We look back on this adventure and discover that we *all* get surprised. It's never the way we think it will go, including whether they'll be boys or girls, biological or adopted, one magical Down's syndrome child, or no biological kids but three international adoptions. We look back on our journey and say, "Wow, I didn't see that coming."

We head off for that fantasy vacation at Wally World with all bags neatly packed, prepared for every eventuality, and then find ourselves holed up in the hotel room riding out the storm of the century, having the time of our lives playing board games and eating vending machine snacks.

Ah, yes! These are the moments that we look back on and say, "Wow, God, I didn't see that coming, but help me remember how incredibly, astoundingly grand it was." We realize that the greatest joy of our small, fleeting adventure is often what happens on the journey rather than the destination. Our agendas are often blown to kingdom come, and all we have is a story. And the story is far more transcendent than our pseudo-sacred agenda that we so carefully crafted in our imagination.

Sometimes it takes car crashes, health crises, diaper disasters, canceled flights, split jeans, and chicken pox to get us to where God wants us to be. And when we get there, we dust ourselves off and do the dance.

My cautious nature, so attracted to spreadsheets, game plans, and satellite navigators, is often reminded that life is a precarious narrative that is intricately woven together in a divine, sometimes dubious, backstory of spiritual adventure. Even the small moments of surprise rise to the surface as signs that we aren't alone. We are being guided by Someone who sees the bigger story and knows exactly what we need. This is the very definition of family—a band of souls brought together through blood, blessing, and bedtimes. We do life together, and we find that there's always a place we can call home. It really doesn't have anything to do with brick and mortar. It's all about love and belonging. Unpredictable? Yes. Unnecessary? Never!

And at the end of the road, with gray heads and crooked smiles, we can look back on it all and say to our beloved family, "Man, I didn't see that coming, but I'm sure glad it came!"

Glory Be Declaration

"What, then, are we to say about these things? If God is for us, who is against us? He did not even spare his own Son but gave him up for us all. How will he not also with him grant us everything?"

(Romans 8:31-31)

PART 4:
Church

Oh-No: This church is full of messed up people.
Aha: I'm one of them!
Glory Be: That's why we need Jesus and each other.

It takes all kinds of churches to reach all kinds of people. I can't wait to get to heaven when we are all together as *the* Church. We won't need special visitor parking spots or welcome stations. We'll just all be there together, for eternity. Its sounds kind of scary until you realize that Jesus will be there too. That one fact puts all the pieces together.

Oh-no, Aha, and Glory Be

Matt Tullos

I Nominate Clara

If I could nominate someone for the most beautiful person in the world, it would be Clara. But she'd never win, because her teeth aren't perfect and she'd scoff at the thought of getting a manicure. She's at least eighty years old and has no concept of what social media is about. She once heard someone mention Snapchat and thought it was a talk show about turtles. She's just a widow in our church from the backwoods of Tennessee with an eighth grade education. But believe me, she's beautiful.

She's been preparing for the next Operation Christmas Child since January, spending days on end looking for a bulk sale on toothbrushes, tiny dolls, and crayons. She pulls every guilt trip in the book to get a lower price from the manager of the dollar store.

To be honest, Clara is one of the bluntest communicators in the church. I remember in '99 when the church went with contemporary music, she set a meeting with the pastor, which scared him half to death. What would she say? With an intimidating scowl on her face, she made her point. "I don't like all this new-fangled, loud, groovy music. I don't like drums, and I certainly prefer the organ, but if that's what it's gonna take to reach my grandkids, all I've got to say is, let's rock!" It wasn't what he was expecting. But that's just Clara.

She once made twenty pans of dressing for Thanksgiving at a homeless shelter. And she did it at home with a thirty-year-old oven. I don't know how she did it, but the fish and loaves provide a biblical precedent for such anomalies.

If someone didn't want to go through the study *Experiencing God*, I would invite them to experience Clara. This summer I was watching a local news feature on a demonstration for racial equality when I did a double take. There she was, Clara, an elderly white lady, marching with the millennials, holding a sign that read, *Jesus is not a Raccist*. (She needed a little editorial assistance on the sign, but everybody knew what she meant.)

During the shortage of PPE in 2020, she took half her dresses and made face masks. I would pass members of the church and think to myself, *That mask looks strangely familiar.*

Clara has never been much of a glamour girl, even when she was in her twenties. Believe me, I've seen the pictures. But when it comes to soul, she's the most beautiful person alive.

Glory Be Declaration

"Serve the Lord with gladness; come before him with joyful songs."

(Psalm 100:2)

You Are Now Entering the Church Visitor Vortex

As we moved to a new town, one of the things we looked forward to experiencing with great excitement—and some fear—was the move to a new church. Like the beginning of the new year, it's a clean, white sheet of paper, just waiting for a new story to be written. A new family in a foreign land.

In most cities, you'll find a variety of churches. Our first church visit was unforgettable. Our car was commandeered by three yellow-vested parking attendants and directed to a visitor's parking spot next to the pregnant mothers' spots. We stepped out of the car and were ushered by two men to the visitors' table. I felt like I was a part of the friendliest abduction ever. We were handed a bag of homemade cookies that still felt gooey and warm, presented with fresh gourmet coffee in a real cup with the church's name on it, and assigned a staff member who filled out the visitor card for us and then escorted us to an assigned seating place. At some point, one of the greeters put a sticker on my back with my first name on it. I really needed to go to the bathroom, but I saw this tall burley looking guy with a security badge, and I decided to just hold it until I could make a clean getaway. I have to admit this church was impressive, although I had vertigo from the moving backgrounds of the slides they used for the worship lyrics. When we returned home, we had another plastic basket with a ton of church-branded gifts like pencils, cup warmers, pocket knives, can openers, and other sanctimonious swag. Plus, there was a large sign in our yard that said, "We just visited *Good Feelin' Community Church!*" (*The name has been changed to protect the fellowship.) We walked in the door as simultaneous text messages and robocalls hit our phones, thanking us for the visit and imploring us to not miss the second installment of the "Wacky Animals in Scripture that Make Us Wish We Owned a Zoo" sermon series.

I really enjoyed it, though. The message was great, and the worship was God focused. We might go back if I can get a handle on the dizziness and puppy-like enthusiasm of the greeters. It's a lot to take on if you are an introvert like me. We have visited other churches, some of them friendly, others low-key and serene, and still others warmly formal. It reminds me that there are lots of different types of churches. I'm glad for them all. It takes all kinds of churches to reach all kinds of people. I can't wait to get to heaven when we are all together as *the* Church. We won't need special visitor parking spots or welcome stations. We'll just all be there together, for eternity. It sounds kind of scary until you realize that Jesus will be there too. That one fact puts all the pieces together.

What questions do you ask of the church family you desire? Here are mine:

- Is the Apostles' Creed the only thing you'll make me sign?
- Do you break bread and pass the cup without the formulaic, once-a-quarter, get-it-over-with attitude?
- Do you woo the homeless woman and the broken addict more than you woo me?
- Is gossip, judgmentalism, and apathy right up there with adultery?
- Are you willing to hold my toes to the fire when I start speaking a line of crap?
- Do you dream big about small things and look for hope rather than blame?
- Do you not end every service by making me hold hands and singing a sappy, unbiblical jingle?
- Are you over the bait and switch invitation phase?
- Do you believe the holy scripture more than you believe the talk show party lines?
- Are you willing to fight for life as a holy thing?
- Do you laugh hysterically and cry unabashedly inside those walls?
- Can you disagree with me without turning it into an emotional event?
- Do you break out in hives when someone says, "business meeting"?
- Will you let my kids be kids and not adults?
- Did you burn the hoops you used to jump through?
- Are you on a pilgrimage for the cross?

Aha Moment

"But you are a chosen race, a royal priesthood, a holy nation, a people for his possession, so that you may proclaim the praises of the one who called you out of darkness into his marvelous light. Once you were not a people, but now you are God's people; you had not received mercy, but now you have received mercy."

(1 Peter 2:9-10)

Oh-No, Aha, and Glory Be

Paint on the Wall

If you grew up in a traditional church culture, you may have experienced a church business meeting. As a minister's kid, I've been to more than I care to remember. My conservative parents never allowed us to watch professional wrestling on TV, so the church business meeting filled a real void in my life. One Wednesday night, during one of those two-hour, smack-down, parliamentary-paloozas, I sat in the back and wrote this little poem:

There once was a church upon a hill
where everything was fine until
the paint inside was getting old
and peeling in some spots, I'm told.

The pastor called a business meeting.
And after the preliminary greeting,
The deacons cried, "Come one! Come all!
What color shall we paint each wall?"

They gathered in the sanctuary,
each determined and contrary.
Sister Gail said, "What do you think
about a very chartreuse pink?"

Brother Dave said to the crowd,
"Isn't that a bit too loud?
I prefer a subtle blue.
It makes the walls look clean and new."

Six women rebuked, "We wanted gold!
It seems much warmer. Blue's too cold!"
A man in the back began to bellow,
"Yellow! Yellow! Yellow! Yellow!"

*The pastor said, "I'm here more than all of you.
I agree with Dave. The walls should be blue."
From that point on their voices grew stronger.
Each emotional plea became longer and longer.*

*Then a voice of strong and stern love
silenced the church as it spoke from above.*

*"You wonder why you can't hear My call
when your greatest struggle is paint on the wall.
Paint your church the pale color of skin.
For you let no other races come in.
Paint your church a wealthy green.
For you ignore starvation that you've seen.
Paint it white and clean as uncalloused feet.
For you refuse to share My joy in the street.
I agree that your walls could be painted in blue,
for your hearts so cold are given to few.
You give many renditions of church as a game,
but you fail to give water in My Holy Name.
You pray using eloquent thees and thous
And yet you forget about the heres and nows.
You struggle to be an earthly saint.
But My love must not be covered in paint."*

Aha Moment

"See! I stand at the door and knock. If anyone hears my voice and opens the door, I will come in to him and eat with him, and he with me."

(Revelation 3:20)

The Most Realistic Christmas Pageant Ever

It wasn't the *Best Christmas Pageant Ever*. They wrote a book about that one and later turned it into a movie. But last year on a dark, moonless night, I went to a Christmas musical in a tiny church nestled around a Louisiana swamp. Google maps isn't too keen on that stretch of land, and I had to stop several times to get directions. Getting directions from people who speak a mixture of broken English and French Creole requires hand signals, the identification of certain cattle breeds near turns, and a bit of dramatization to describe the landmarks.

The little Baptist church was packed because Catholics like a good show, and there were too many sacred things to knock over in their massive, pristine Cathedral fifteen miles away. Baptist churches are a little more durable, as long as someone doesn't knock the cardboard Lottie Moon Offering display into the baptistry. When I arrived, the cars were everywhere; I had to park in the street. I wasn't worried. This church was the only reason anyone would need to travel down this doglegged, bayou-hugging road. This was sasquatch country. I was told that no one in this area puts any life-sized Santa sleigh displays near their homes. It's deer season, and people have had their windows accidentally shot out by confused hunters.

The church could seat one hundred people, but there must have been one hundred thirty in attendance. It was a strange mixture of people—a virtual gumbo-pot of all races, tribes, and tongues. I walked in and felt a strange moisture running up my ankle. A miniature goat was chewing off a part of my sock. Evidently I had entered in time for the procession of the shepherds. The whiff of live animals hung in the air, and I stood for the entirety of the program and watched people of all ages filling the roles of wisemen crowned with colanders wrapped in foil, angels with coat hanger halos, and others in their most biblical-looking bathrobes and sandals.

At the end, we all cheered, which scared baby Jesus half to death. It sounded as if we had seen *Hamilton* on Broadway. Oh, this was much more important than a Broadway show. This was the celebration of the greatest gift we'd ever been given. The evening was perfect, but not because the program was perfect. It was perfect because we had seen a glimpse of Advent: God coming down to messy, broken, multicultural people surrounded by animals, children, and angels.

Glory Be Declaration

"For a child will be born for us, a son will be given to us, and the government will be on his shoulders. He will be named Wonderful Counselor, Mighty God, Eternal Father, Prince of Peace."

(Isaiah 9:6)

Matt Tullos

Doorbells and the Cloak of Shame

A part of sanity is being able to identify your insanity. For me, it's the doorbell. As a frequently messy family, we are frozen by that infrequent chime. We treat it with suspicion and foreboding doom. We are overwhelmed by the implications of someone, anyone (even a sales rep) possibly seeking an actual face-to-face conversation with us. Or, what's worse, it could be someone we actually admire. It might be our pastor or small group leader coming to drop off a gift, which automatically behooves one to say, "Come on in!" A person bearing gifts must be invited in. It's in Leviticus. I'm almost positive.

For our family, the subtext of the phrase, *Come on in*, is often, *Come on in and forgive the sock sorting project on the couch, the pizza boxes from the late-night supper after the youth event, the small rocket-propelled t-shirt-flinging device our son is repairing in the foyer, and the escaped ferret that could be anywhere. If we would have been given fifteen minutes' notice of your arrival, everything would be stuffed in closets, and we'd have tea and crumpets in the sunroom, with Kari Jobe's latest song playing softly in the background.* That's the picture we'd love for you to see.

I must, hereby, confess my love of masks. I wish I could be seen as the neat, organized, normal guy who has it all together, but that just isn't the case. Between me and you, our world looks *exactly* like that every year . . . for about two minutes and thirty seconds. This is not a critique of things being beautiful. I would much rather see *home as artwork* in a magazine than *home as health hazard!* And so would you. But we must give ourselves permission to confess that life—everybody's life—gets messy from time to time. We all have our struggles, our freak-out moments, our "who burned the cat's tail?" discoveries, and "what's that smell?" mysteries. *Everybody* has them.

Finally, after many years of diligently trying to measure up to our self-imposed reputation, Darlene and I are learning to embrace our imperfect, messy world and realize that the more vulnerable we are around others the more God can use our story. To pretend perfection is just dead religion. Yes, my wife and I need to do the deep cleaning of our baseboards and the organizational symmetry of our storage room, but we're working harder on being open, present, and mindful of the things that matter most.

One day I hope I'll be so recovered from the usual cloak of shame that I'll be delighted to hear the doorbell ring. I'm not there yet, but I'm working on it.

Glory Be Declaration

"Keeping our eyes on Jesus, the pioneer and perfecter of our faith. For the joy that lay before him, he endured the cross, despising the shame, and sat down at the right hand of the throne of God."

(Hebrews 12:2)

Armadillos Saved Me

It was my worst mistake in leading youth at a church, and it was my first mistake. As a college freshman, I was a youth minister at a small country church in the wilderness of north Louisiana. We had about five students that came regularly to the church. And what would be my first activity? A lock-in, of course. If you are new to the term, it's where you keep a mixed group of teenagers awake all night with crazy games, scavenger hunts, and massive amounts of caffeine and carbohydrates. It's actually been banned in fifteen states. (Not really, but it should be. Especially for nineteen-year-old rookie youth ministers.) For me, it seemed like a good idea at the time.

"Can we invite friends?" my five students asked.

"Why, of course!" I replied with the zeal of Peter at Pentecost. I thought my five students would bring a couple of extra friends. I also announced it on Sunday and invited adults to attend. A couple of senior adults nodded their heads and smiled from the pews, so I took that as a, *Yes. I'll help*. (Do you see the two trains heading toward each other on the same track? I thought so.)

It started on a Friday night after the high school football game, and half the high school showed up. I had stupidly written down five games, rented a movie, and prepared a brief devotional to utilize. Somehow, I must have thought that the football game would go into triple overtime, or I greatly over-estimated my impromptu creativity. No other adults showed up, and by the time it was 1 a.m., I was completely out of game ideas, movie thrills, adult supervision, and junk food. The train wreck was in beast mode, and I was on the verge of panic. What do you do with one hundred students and no rational adults at a church that was three hundred miles away from the closest all-night bowling alley?

We went outside at around 2 a.m. The kids were bored out of their minds. Suddenly, like manna from heaven, a flock of armadillos migrated across an adjacent field. All the students' eyes widened. They grabbed flashlights from the church, and the chase was on. Evidently this was a thing in these parts—chasing armadillos.

Looking back on it, I don't understand how someone didn't get a broken leg or rabies, but time passed swiftly. It had everything: adventure, wildlife, danger, and teamwork. To this day, when I see an armadillo on a road, I hit the brakes and skirt around it. Their ancestors saved me years ago.

Glory Be Declaration

"Now to him who is able to do above and beyond all that we ask or think according to the power that works in us."

(Ephesians 3:20)

Matt Tullos

Groupthink Makes Stink

Groupthink without God is a dangerous proposition. I'm seeing a lot of groupthink in the culture these days. *Groupthink* is often defined as thinking or making decisions as a group in a way that discourages personal responsibility.

These days, whenever something has been re-tweeted thirty thousand times, you are seeing groupthink. Whenever millions of people are catapulted into ecstasy by a three-hundred-pound guy barreling down a striped field with an oblong ball, you're seeing groupthink. But groupthink goes back all the way to the Old Testament.

We see groupthink happening in the wilderness right after Israel witnesses the most impressive miracles since the creation of the female. Seas part! Sticks turn into snakes! Frogs! Locusts! Water gushing out of rocks! And before, during, and after all this amazingness, they usually complained. *Why didn't you just leave us in stinking Egypt! At least we'd have onions and leaks to eat. Because who doesn't like onions and leaks roasted in a goat-dung-fueled outdoor oven.* (Of course, that's my personal paraphrase.)

Groupthink is best used by complainers, and the Israelites were especially gifted in complaining. They complained about no meat, too much meat, that it was too difficult to go into the Promised Land, weak leadership, too assertive leadership, no water, bitter water. Moses was so exasperated by all that Yiddish groupthink that in Numbers 11:15, he basically reaches a breaking point as he cries out to God, "If you are going to treat me like this, please kill me right now if I have found favor with you, and don't let me see my misery anymore." In other words, *Just shoot me!*

A few centuries later, David saw groupthink when he was delivering pizza (or at least bread and cheese) to his brothers. The groupthink was, *Are you crazy? You think God's army should fight? There's this one guy that's really tall. I mean, he's like 9'9", and he's got a wicked flying pig tattoo! Totally un-kosher! We dare not fight this one singular ogre!* That is groupthink. It produces golden calves, selling brothers, jealous kings, Babel towers, and doubting disciples.

And we aren't immune to groupthink. There can be groupthink in churches when the thermostat isn't managed properly and people are sweltering in sizzling seventy-three-degree temperatures. There's groupthink when the people stand silently and cross their arms during worship on Sunday. And there's groupthink when we avoid talking about important stuff when we get together. Groupthink is what you get when people avoid the Bible, focus on their appetites only, and tackle the big issues through collective dude-brainstorming. As men, we have to groupthink differently.

Oh-No Admonition

"Therefore I, the prisoner in the Lord, urge you to walk worthy of the calling you have received, with all humility and gentleness, with patience, bearing with one another in love, making every effort to keep the unity of the Spirit through the bond of peace."

(Ephesians 4:1-3)

Oh-No, Aha, and Glory Be

Letting God Out of the Box

*I'm always amazed how the church as a whole
is so quick to throw rocks at the sheep in the fold.
We question each other's theology,
spar over worship philosophy.
We've got more fusses than one tongue can tell,
while outside the world is going to hell.
We are driven by creeds and motions and clocks;
haven't we learned not to put God in a box?
Would Jesus approve of our political labels,
or would He come in and start busting up tables?
Does He tire of us telling Him what He should do,
what gender must teach, what strategy's true?
Is the Bible the life source or inflexible judge?
Is the church a haven for sinners or a group with a grudge?
Do we think we can settle for boycotts and strife
instead of seeking the lost and giving dead people life?
What were we thinking when in front of the press
we majored on minors choosing to curse and not bless.
I have to tell you from my point of view,
I keep wondering what in the world Jesus would do.
Would He have us disputing which method is best
or making transformation be our holy quest?
After all, that's what this journey's about,
not who has more sheep or who has more clout.
I despise the reports of our ugly catfights.
I'm appalled by the task of reading sinners their rights.
When you preach condemnation, consider this fact:
they don't know Jesus. How'd you expect them to act?
And please understand, I'm not where I should be.*

Matt Tullos

When I'm preaching at you, I'm preaching at me.
There are times when I haven't lived up to His name,
when I've only the man in the mirror to blame.
But now is the time to reject the mask,
to heed the call, and get back to the task.
To burn the political, decaying façade
for an all-out pursuit of our passionate God.
Let's spend our time living meaningful lives,
giving mercy to sinners not dangerous lies.
Let's bear the cross and drop the rocks,
proclaim the good news and let God out of the box.

Oh-No Admonition

"So tell the people, 'This is what the LORD of Armies says: Return to me—this is the declaration of the LORD of Armies—and I will return to you, says the LORD of Armies.'"

(Zechariah 1:3)

The Art of Lingo

Over the years I've worked in lots of positions, most of them revolving around churches and Christian organizations. It can really be a fishbowl, but I keep up with the outside world vicariously through church leaders, publishers, professors, and other successful men and women in the business world. Thanks to them, I'm learning the lingo.

The other day, when talking about our need for a food pantry in our church, a team leader said, "I think we need to *drill down* to *leverage* our *core competency* and see if we have *buy-in* because we always seem to work out of *silos,* and lots of people think we should just *stay in our lane.*" I was speechless. It was obvious that I was in over my head. I felt like the disciples in Luke 18:34: "They did not understand any of this. Its meaning was hidden from them, and they did not know what he was talking about."

I proceeded to google the words and realized that I was way behind the times. So I added business terms to my marital lexicon and experimented with my wife:

"I'd mow the grass, but I need to *stay in my lane* and *leverage* the *core competency* of our son. I'll *vision cast* it with him and see if I get any *buy-in* so that he might come out of his room . . . I mean *silo.*"

This did not compute. Darlene immediately asked what medication I might have taken for my sinus infection. We all have lingo that we pick up through the years. Churches are particularly versed at this. We have phrases like,

- *That hurt my heart:* Do not call the cardiologist.
- *I want to share something with you:* Watch out. This might be gossip.
- *The Fellowship Hall:* Not a hall. It's an ancient term for the room where casseroles are dispensed.
- *Bless his heart:* In other words, *I'm trying to be nice, but he's clueless. Somebody help him!*
- *The Committee on Committees:* Um . . . I'm still trying to figure out that one.
- *Extended Session:* Another ancient vernacular developed some time in the 1600s. It's used primarily by church staff, referring to the place where the kids go during worship and the one ministry in the church that is never overstaffed.

Oh-No Admonition

"But avoid irreverent babble, for it will lead people into more and more ungodliness."

(2 Timothy 2:16)

Metaphorical lingo is good, but for people like me, it is fraught with ambiguity, so I'm trying to use it sparingly. And I don't test them out on my wife. So today I think I'll just walk over to his room and tell him that the grass is getting high, and if he wants to use the car tonight, he'll have to mow and edge. That's the business lingo he'll truly understand.

PART 5:
Random Observations

Oh-No: What's the deal with this?
Aha: So that's the deal with that!
Glory Be: I see the Divine in every detail.

We'll understand it better, by and by. But when we get to the by and by, I don't think I'll care that much about any of those mysteries. Greater mysteries are to come.

Oh-No, Aha, and Glory Be

We Meet Again, Beloved Extended Family

Thanksgiving is a celebration of distant yet connected families coming together. It's also a great time to be thankful that we don't live under the same roof with *all* our cousins, aunts, uncles, and great-half-stepfathers. There's a reason we only eat cranberry sauce once or twice a year. It's a novelty best enjoyed after long intervals. There are personalities and family types that show up in almost every family gathering, maybe even in your family.

You have the cousin who hugs you like he's your best friend and immediately starts in on you: "I've been thinking about you. I just stumbled across a new venture that could not only be the beginning of financial freedom but a chance to spend time living the life you want to live. I'd love to spend the next ten hours sharing this incredible opportunity with you. I even brought a flip chart!" It's awkward on many levels. Multi-levels to be exact.

Back when I was a kid, I had one phobia. It was the hug from one of my long since gone to glory step-great-grandmothers. She had a mole on her cheek with one hair sticking out that was sharper than a straight pin. I'd see her coming my way, knowing that she would be pressing that one hair deep into my right cheek. It felt like a measles shot, and I feared it would leave a scar just like that vaccination did on my arm.

Almost every family has the super awkward political guy. He mistakes the table for a spicy segment on *Meet the Press*. He comes to the meal loaded for bear. He's memorized over three hundred political memes he's gleaned from social media and is sure that pilgrims invited the Indians to dinner in order to persuade them that the Mayor of Jamestown was an oaf.

Most extended families have at least one "perfect family." They're the ones with the whitest teeth, the fanciest cars, and success in all things. They arrive for Thanksgiving bearing their Christmas letter which, of course, they had printed much earlier. It includes pictures of their summer in Paris and ten thousand words about the amazing achievements of all three kids. They sashay into your home with the grace of angels—impressive and to be envied. But you might end up seeing them arguing with each other in the car as they pull out of your drive.

Oh-No, Aha, and Glory Be

And of course, there's a guy like me. Spookily quiet, observing and enjoying the chaos. I have plenty of personality picadilloes of my own. Believe me, I am as dysfunctional as they come. But I've learned a few charm school tips: nod politely, listen more than you talk, and take really good notes. As a writer, there's lots of material at these gatherings. If your family seems to have more than its share of dysfunction, it's encouraging to remember that God has been using dysfunctional families for thousands of years. Just read the Bible, and you'll find lots of works in progress around this grand table called grace.

Oh-No Admonition

"So then, let us pursue what promotes peace and what builds up one another."
(Romans 14:19)

Matt Tullos

No Worries? Yes Worries!

My wife is married to a guy with too much information. She's out of town, but I know exactly where she is as long as she doesn't turn her phone off. The "Find My Wife" app (as she affectionately calls it) shows me on a map exactly where she is. It's my favorite app. Maybe it's the fear of abandonment. But the truth is, I love knowing exactly where the people I love are located at all times. For some reason, my sons hate it and have denied my request to allow me to track them as well. Who cares that they are over twenty-one? I simply love their face on a map. What if they get abducted? They get it, but they are beginning to suspect that my issues go much deeper.

You see, I am a bit of a worrier. I always have been. It's not something that I'm particularly proud to say, but if I watch an hour of Fox News or CNN, I can convince myself that I have a rare, newly discovered disease, while identity thieves are stealing my 401K, which is irrelevant because a nuclear bomb could well be rocketing my direction, and if that doesn't kill us, the irritable bowel possibilities in the future are *endless*.

Yes. I can worry about all that at the same time. I'm a *worry multi-tasker* . . . a hoarder of fret fodder. Really. So I stick with the standard thirty-minute network news.

So, dear Lester Holt: When I come home, just give me a few headlines and that last story at the end to inspire me or cause me to gush over the cuteness of rescued basset hound puppies. Please, Lester, kill me with cute rather than the inevitable Ebola outbreak. Otherwise I might be in the master closet wearing homemade aluminum foil headgear. I don't think ignorance is bliss. But ultimately I'm trying to learn the groove of gratitude and trust. My worry is slowly being replaced with something else.

Instead of worrying, I will,

- Love relentlessly.
- Never let anything stand between me and my wife.
- Celebrate the little things.
- Say important, loving words because, in truth, we are never promised tomorrow.
- Control my work; spend the night with my spouse (not the other way around).
- Constantly invest in relationships.
- Learn to forgive, forgive, and forgive. It truly is divine!
- Admit my hurts and faults.
- Listen with my ears, my eyes, and my heart.
- Trust God with every detail that is out of my control.
- And last but not least . . . never, ever give up on my wife—even when the app can't find her.

Oh-No Admonition

"Therefore I tell you: Don't worry about your life, what you will eat or what you will drink; or about your body, what you will wear. Isn't life more than food and the body more than clothing?"

(Matthew 6:25)

Vans and Me

A while back we said farewell to our last minivan. Although my wife waxed philosophically about all the good times our family shared roaming the interstates while our kids were younger, I silently celebrated the occasion. It's not that I yearned for a candy apple red midlife crisis convertible. I've just had a few harrowing experiences with vans.

As I watched the young couple set sail in our last minivan, I remembered that time we were driving in a torrential downpour on I-40 when our van went into a spin. I don't mean hydroplaning. I mean a multi-revolution, high-speed, gyroscope stunt that Scott Hamilton and Kristi Yamaguchi would have envied. I remember my wife, Darlene, who was feeding our newborn in the back seat, had time to get the baby secured in the car seat and check on the other three boys and then fasten her own seatbelt before the spin cycle was over. We ended the maneuver right side up and headed in the right direction in the same lane we started in. People passed us on the interstate, looking into our van with disbelief. God was with me that day. It wasn't funny at the time, but it is a legendary van tale in our family.

And before I had kids, I had some pretty scary times in vans. While I was in seminary, I worked as a jailer at Euless City Jail between Dallas and Fort Worth. As a part of my job, I transferred inmates from the city jail to the county jail. On an especially windy Tuesday afternoon, I was transferring the female prisoners. There is a certain amount of protocol to the job that I had followed for months. It was second nature, or so I thought. I pulled up to the Tarrant County facility, got out, unlocked the rear door where the inmates were, and released their seatbelts (since they were handcuffed). In the middle of the process, a Texas gale slammed the door shut. Because there was no internal lock-release, I found myself (you guessed it) locked in the van with the inmates. It took several minutes to persuade someone that I was a jailer and not a felon. And after my rescue, I became the favorite story of the Euless City headquarters. I was the seminary student who locked himself in a van with the female felons. My new nickname was "Windshear."

I have plenty of other van stories. I backed a church van into a motel on a mission trip. I lost a van at a mall with all four kids in tow when I took them Christmas shopping for Mom. I clipped a deer in our van on a Christmas journey. The kids thought it was a reindeer. But I am silent on the issue. I got into the wrong van at a grocery store and didn't realize it until my key wouldn't work, and I noticed the confused owners peering in the driver's window. We went through three vans and three hundred thousand miles as we traveled down the unpredictable, complicated road of parenthood. Extra angels were assigned to me through the years because it's a miracle we made it through the journey of parenthood without a single scrape. God's providence made up for my ineptitude, and I am wiser for the experience.

I have to smile when I pass a van on the interstate with the latest Disney movie running on their flip-down TV screens and remember all the wonderful and treacherous moments of family travel. I envy them for a moment. Just a moment . . . and then I whisper a prayer of thanksgiving.

Glory Be Declaration

"The Lord is the one who will go before you. He will be with you; he will not leave you or abandon you. Do not be afraid or discouraged."

(Deuteronomy 31:8)

Aging Thirty Years in Half a Second

Last week, I did the annual spring cleaning. I love getting rid of stuff. Like most, it happens on a warm Saturday afternoon after the garage sale. We sold 174 items and ended up with around thirty-five dollars. I was amazed that so many people don't want what *we* don't want. By the end of the day, I was paying people to take what was left over. *I'll pay you fifty dollars to take the sofa that's parked in the garage. Please? I know it's mauve. But mauve is back! I'll even throw in the inflatable Santa Claus!*

After a Saturday of lifting a refrigerator, an entertainment center, my son's barbells, and various other items, I woke up the next morning and grabbed a shirt out of the closet, and the next thing I knew, a shock of electricity shot through my back. I aged thirty years in half a second as I tried to get up. I looked at myself in the mirror—it was a pathetic sight. I was stooped down and to the right at a sixty-degree angle. I had the posture of the Elephant Man. What happened? The day before, I was robust, vigorous, and almost impressed with the deftness of my herculean prowess—and the next, I'm bent over like an extra on the set of the *Golden Girls* after attempting the feat of lifting a shirt from the closet. I went to church like that because I didn't have time to draft a small group leader replacement. Our group was very understanding and prayed for my restoration, but evidently these demons require much prayer and fasting.

Monday, I found a chiropractor who could squeeze me into the schedule. I am not a frequenter of chiropractors, but I've been before. I've learned through the years that there are different schools of thought when it comes to chiropractors. (Or as my grandmother called them, "the choir-practors.") Some of them have a little tool that pokes you in the spine after they hook you up to something akin to an octopus with electrical suction cups. I've been to others that wanted to sign me up for a lifetime supply of supplements containing things like lamb's hair extract, acacia seeds, and aromatic wild caught salmon oil. For me, I don't think you've actually been to a chiropractor until he puts you on a plank of wood and you hear bones popping as he plunges his knee in your thoracic vertebrae. That's when I know I got my money's worth.

It's been a few days, and I'm walking normally now. I've learned a lot since then. I've learned that it's the little things that often trigger the hidden pain of over-exertion. I think that's true in marriage. It's often not the actual disagreements we have that bend Darlene and me out of shape. It's sometimes the guy tailgating me on the way home that incites my contrarian mindset. And sometimes the best thing I can do to keep my marriage and my back healthy is a little daily stretching. It's not as macho as weightlifting, but it's just as important.

Glory Be Declaration

"Come to me, all of you who are weary and burdened, and I will give you rest."

(Matthew 11:28)

Matt Tullos

I Ain't Afraid of No Ghosting

It occurred to me the other day that dating has gone Old Testament on us. Well, sort of. There are now arranged marriages again! But marriages aren't arranged by the parents; they are arranged by the internet. It seems like every young, starry-eyed engaged couple found each other on Facebook or one of the many assorted and precarious dating apps. One reality show even matches couples to be married sight unseen! Really?

I am, of course, skeptical. To me, the internet isn't like a wise old father arranging star-crossed lovers with pinpoint accuracy. Father Internet is more like that crazy uncle with horrible eyesight who gives unsolicited advice at Thanksgiving and has the judgement of a fifteen-year-old student driver in rush hour traffic. I've heard some success stories, though, and I have friends that met their husband or wife on a dating site. My son, who's in the Army, met a wonderful girl. She loves the Lord and has a great family, and we have grown to really like her. The only problem is that she doesn't speak English. Not a word! We communicate through a translate smartphone app. I have great hopes that she might be *the* one, but the communication must improve. That's the big hurdle, right?

I'm kind of an old soul. I just met my wife in a Sunday school class. We never swiped right or left, whatever that means. Swiping a girl sounds like what a friend of mine did with my prom date. He swiped her right out from under my nose. I'm still recovering emotionally from that romantic petty thief.

Another son of mine told me it had been a tough week because he got "ghosted." *Got ghosted?* I didn't even know that was a verb. He explained that *ghosted* is when a girl drops off the grid and doesn't text back. It's evidently a thing these days.

Everyone is afraid of hard conversations. But I don't blame these young'uns. I never liked the, "It's not you, it's me" break-up meetings. I'd be ghosting right along with the best of them. It just makes me glad I made it out of the singles department early. I'm praying my four sons get married before they are fifty. By that time, I think I'll be mature enough to be a grandfather.

Oh-No Admonition

"Then we will no longer be little children, tossed by the waves and blown around by every wind of teaching, by human cunning with cleverness in the techniques of deceit. But speaking the truth in love, let us grow in every way into him who is the head—Christ."

(Ephesians 4:14-15)

A Moving Experience

We recently moved into a new house, and I have to say that I'm over moving. Completely over it. I will not move again unless I see a burning bush or Bigfoot or if Eminem frequently rents the house next door for block parties. I'm just no good at it. I don't know how to pack a truck. I usually end up saying something really stupid to my wife, which entails a second move—to the dog house.

It's fairly easy to spot a guy in the middle of a move. He's the one wearing the ripped cargo pants, walking around in a daze with a limp, combing the dark alleys between stores for free boxes. But at first glance, you might mistake him as a homeless man with really nice tennis shoes.

This time I was so exhausted after loading that I hired two men from Craigslist to help me unload. That was humiliating. I lifted the rental truck gate, and a barrage of items tumbled out like a bad round of Jenga. "Who packed this thing?" one of the Craigslist guys asked. I just chuckled, embarrassed and somewhat emasculated. "I know. I was in a rush. Kind of a 'Passover in the middle of the night' deal." They just stared back, confused. I guess their acumen for Old Testament history is somewhat like my skill for tying knots, appliance dollies, and using the pillows to cushion the china cabinets. In the end, they pitied me, and I tipped them well.

Of course, with all moves, a new domicile always requires new paint. *Why did we buy a house with such high ceilings?* It's so roomy, so spacious, so gallant, and yet *so* deadly for the amateur husband perched in impossible locations. My wife came in, and I was sitting on top of kitchen cabinets, painting in my underwear. It seemed odd, I'm sure. I explained my two fears; it was a real dilemma: I don't want to get paint on my clothes, but I also didn't want to be in my underwear when the ambulance arrived. What's a man to do? Later my wife bought me a jumpsuit. Great. Now I'm even prepared for prison.

I don't believe in purgatory, but if there was such a place, I am convinced that it would consist of entering the afterlife with all your possessions and being forced to move back and forth from Yankton, South Dakota, to Cisco, Texas, in a beat-up truck with no packing tape, newspapers, or wardrobe boxes, until you did it without breaking a figurine.

Aha Moment

"Sell your possessions and give to the poor. Make money-bags for yourselves that won't grow old, an inexhaustible treasure in heaven, where no thief comes near and no moth destroys. For where your treasure is, there your heart will be also."

(Luke 12:33-34)

Matt Tullos

I'm So Glad I'm Not a Girl

The greatest gift I have ever been given was on my wedding day. I was given the blessing of a partner that would walk through all the stages of my life with me—the better and the worse, the sickness and the health, and eventually the "death do us part." I know. That last vow is a morbid and grammatically perplexing thing to think about on the most dressed up occasion of your life. I've learned lots about how different males and females are. The differences are far greater than the plumbing we have preinstalled in our hardware. Here are a few:

> *Women have lots more applications.* For instance, shampoo. I thought about it as I showered this morning and stared at the fifteen bottles of hair products and my all-in-one hair and body wash. Then I walked into the closet and measured out fifteen yards of female clothing options on hangers compared to my three feet. I realized again that women have a whole lot more going on in the "getting ready" category. This is not a new thing. Esther 2 describes the world record for getting ready for a date. She went through twelve months of beauty treatments prescribed for the women: six months with oil of myrrh and six with perfumes and cosmetics. That's a whole lot more than fifteen bottles of hair care products in the shower and thirty minutes of getting ready for our small group Bible study. So no, this trend didn't start with the advent of Instagram selfies.
>
> *Most guys I know are just basic dudes.* Five pairs of shoes—max, greeting cards with ten words or less, terse responses during conflict, and three documents or less on our computer desktop. Before I married, I described yellow as *yellow*. Since then, I have discovered canary, gold, Tuscan sun, dijon, banana, blonde, pineapple, amber, and honey.

I can see God's hand in it all. I'm learning about feelings, interior design that doesn't involve a singing fish plaque or milk crates, and the wisdom of making sure your belt and shoes match. But infinitely greater than those things, I've also learned about tenderness, intercessory prayer, and compassion. We're still different, though. I can get my hair cut for ten bucks with a coupon and get out in ten minutes flat.

Glory Be Declaration

"For just as the body is one and has many parts, and all the parts of that body, though many, are one body— so also is Christ."

(1 Corinthians 12:12)

Oh-no, Aha, and Glory Be

Matt Tullos

My Stocked-Up Grandma

My grandma always figured a pandemic would happen. I can just see her now, putting down her needlework next to Martha, Ruth, and Eunice in the great sewing circle of heaven, shouting down to me, *I told you that you needed to keep five thousand potatoes in the crawl space under your house!* I always wondered as a kid why she did things like that. I wonder no longer. She always stocked up for the apocalypse. That country lady knew how to survive, and she would have done just fine in 2020. A quarantine wouldn't bother her in the least.

She and my grandfather were never people of means. They never went out to eat. Why do that? No one knew how to cook cornbread, fried okra, field peas, and collard greens like she did. She was organic without even knowing it. And of course, if the cupboard was empty, there were always plenty of potatoes under the house. She survived with no Wi-Fi or Bluetooth. It's amazing how well she got around without all the creature comforts we have today.

We've been getting a taste of primitive living. In March of 2020, we almost resorted to using newspapers and catalogs for toilet paper like she did. Social distancing would be easy for my grandparents. The coronavirus would have a tough time trying to contact them. They lived down a winding gravel road in the middle of a north Louisiana forest. You'd have to go over ten cattle gaps to make it to their door. Yes, cattle gaps. It was a thing. Google it. My time with her was always a feast for the senses: squirrel gumbo, wood stoves, real butter, canned figs, and something called mercurochrome (which is banned by the FDA now). I'm amazed that she lived to ninety. I guess fresh veggies cancels out mercury poisoning. I never feared bullying, pandemics, or cyberattacks. Those things didn't exist in Dry Prong, Louisiana. But I *did* have concerns about Bigfoot.

Times were a whole lot simpler there. But who knows? We might return to them soon. We don't know what the future holds. I might need to purchase a milk cow for the backyard in the coming months if the homeowners' association allows it. But when life slows down, there's always some beauty that rises to the surface. My grandparents were dirt poor, but they were surrounded by wonder. And that's a pretty good trade-off. It's amazing how rich life becomes when you're thankful for simple things like God's grace, running water, a good meal, and lots of time with the people you love most.

Aha Moment

"But godliness with contentment is great gain. For we brought nothing into the world, and we can take nothing out."
(1 Timothy 6:6-7)

That Guy in the Community

The other day I was at a t-ball game. My t-ball days have long since passed. My kids are much older now. A guy I work with had a son playing, and he invited me. I thought it would be fun to revisit those fun years for an hour. So I brushed off the cobwebs on my LSU lawn chair that hadn't been used since the t-ball season of 2003 and drove to the local field of dreams that was thick with younger dads, moms, and kids with fresh uniforms and gloves.

Ah, yes! Spring sprang!

I wondered if *the guy* would be there. When I say *the guy*, I mean the one that is in almost every little league in America from Portland, Maine, to Portland, Oregon. He's got the old baseball cap from his high school days. He is constantly consulting the coach and pelting the umpires with insults and insane credulities. Wherever a ball is being kicked, caught, or shot, he's there. And this evening, he showed up loud, proud, and inconsolable.

I said to my friend, "What's with the dude in the purple shirt and the orange hat?"

"I know, right?" he chuckled. "And get this. He's on the praise team at my church!"

"I thought as a civilization we had gotten past the idea of treating t-ball games like an elimination game of the World Series."

"Well, Dorothy, you aren't in upward t-ball anymore," he replied.

I thought to myself, *I don't ever want to be* that *guy. I don't want to be the guy who takes something that is supposed to be about the kids and makes it all about me.* There are other *that guy* people who are dads:

- I don't want to be *that guy* that makes the mom be responsible for having the important talks while my main responsibility at family gatherings is slathering the ribs with sauce.
- I don't want to be *that guy* that is constantly criticizing the church leaders and rarely taking responsibility for his own spiritual growth.
- I don't want to be *that guy* that sneaks around doing embarrassing things to the demise of his family.

I don't want to be *that guy* who follows and tailgates another vehicle who cut in front of him in heavy traffic. I must confess that it has been a temptation. But I don't like that guy. Nobody does. *Nobody.*

I don't want to be *that guy* that only prays with his family before meals.

And I definitely don't want to be *that guy* that explodes on his family after a hard day in the office.

That's not what I want to be. I have my fair share of parental blunders, and my life is totally a work in progress. But I have a choice, and so do you! *Don't be that guy!*

Oh-No Admonition

"A fool gives full vent to his anger, but a wise person holds it in check."

(Proverbs 29:11)

It's a Year-Round Thing

We recently purchased my dream home, and it's not because it is bigger or better than the seven other homes we've purchased over the past thirty years. This is my dream home because it's right next to the place where I work. I walk to work every day, and I love it. My, how things changed! When you're a kid, driving to a job is living the dream, and now it's *not* hopping in the car for a number of days that makes me feel like I've arrived. It's so much safer than avoiding the texting motorists and roundabouts and negotiating four-way stops. Although, I must confess, I've collided into a number of mailboxes and real estate signs while texting and walking.

The house came with a pool—an unexpected perk. But I'm finding that a pool in the backyard is akin to owning a truck. Friends come out of the woodwork. With a high-strength, military-grade, aluminum-alloy, Ford super-duty truck, you're invited to participate in the transport of every friend's couch purchase. With a pool, you are the host of every ten-year-old's summer birthday party. It's really fun, but it's also a job that requires lots of time and a certain set of chemistry skills acquired over the course of several years. In the Deep South, pool maintenance is important, even in January! Last spring, I had one of those crazy months where the warm days snuck up on me, and I was too busy to notice. I began to hear the sounds of toads at night around the pool. Who knew that when you don't put the chemicals in the pool, lily pads, water bugs, and unidentified swimming objects swiftly take up residence?
In Louisiana, it happens. Quickly. But I managed to do the work, and the green disappeared quickly. I was astounded by the swift change that took place with the right chemicals, leaf removal, and vacuuming. The pool went from "swamp thing" to crystal blue in forty-eight hours!

My pool is a spiritual reminder. If I am not daily, consistently, even *ruthlessly* working on my relationship with Jesus, my wife, and my kids, these relationships will deteriorate quickly. We all have a choice: strength, consistency, and purity, or a jumbo-sized man-made pool of eww! And who wants that when friends come over to your house?

So, in a minute, I'm heading to the pool store to get more calcium, chlorine, and clarifier, and a new pool skimmer to capture that one stubborn, tenacious, *loud* remaining frog. But first, I'm going to finish Ephesians.

Oh-No Admonition

"How can a young man keep his way pure? By keeping your word. I have sought you with all my heart; don't let me wander from your commands."

(Psalm 119:9-10)

Matt Tullos

Joseph, You Got Me There

If there was a Christmas photo on the first morning after Jesus's birth, I would imagine there would be a man in the background photobombing the baby picture. He would look a little frazzled, almost in a daze, but immensely proud of his bride. His name would be Joseph.

When our first child was born, I escorted my wife in an air-conditioned donkey (also known as a Civic) and made a quick five-minute drive at seventy-five miles per hour. Joseph's trip to the birthing room was seventy-five miles without the aid of fossil fuel. *Joseph, you got me there.*

When we arrived, we were assisted by a highly skilled doctor, five nurses, and lots of sterile equipment. Joseph, if not totally alone, may have had the help of a goat, a cow, a camel, and a couple of unemployed shepherds. *Joseph, you got me there.*

My wife was administered a needle in the back called an epidural. This relieved the labor pains. Joseph? No such luck. I almost fainted when our son began to crown. I am a sissy when it comes to my wife in pain. Joseph must have felt the same feelings of panic, helplessness, and sheer terror. I had friends around me to support me. Joseph? He was alone in a town of strangers who could help him find a place to do this whole *Son of God, Immanuel getting born* thing. *Joseph, you got me there.*

My responsibility was simple. All I had to do was timed breathing; supply ice chips; and say encouraging, non-boneheaded words to my wife while manning the phone. Joseph had it *all*, including managing complete strangers visiting shortly after he cut the cord. Once again, *Joseph, you got me there too.*

If the angels took any photos of that first morning for Jesus, I hope we get to see them. I'll be looking for that man who should have won *Dad of the Year 0001 AD*. His life was overshadowed by this Child and his bride. I think that's how we all should be—working behind the scenes and being at the right place at the right time. Woody Allen was right: "Eighty percent of life is just showing up." Joseph added another thirty percent. He gave it the proverbial one hundred ten percent, and he gave us all a picture of an amazing dad.

Glory Be Declaration

"After they were gone, an angel of the Lord appeared to Joseph in a dream, saying, 'Get up! Take the child and his mother, flee to Egypt, and stay there until I tell you. For Herod is about to search for the child to kill him.'"

(Matthew 2:13)

The Sigh Says It All

Social scientists have noted that only seven percent of our messages are in the words that we say. Nonverbal communication is kind of a big deal. I think that would be especially true for guys because wives say about ninety-three percent more words than husbands in a typical marriage. But I think it's true for *both* husbands and wives. It's been said that the Eskimo-Aleut people group have a whole flurry of words for snow. Similarly, there are a myriad of different types of sighs.

For instance, there's a big difference between the exhausted sigh and the exasperated sigh. The exhausted sigh requires your eyelids to be at half-mass and your shoulders to have a slight slump. It's the sigh where you've just left Chuck E. Cheese and you feel like you might collapse once the ringing in your ear from the ski-ball machines diminishes from your consciousness. The exasperated sigh requires a subtle shaking of the head and rolling of the eyes. You perform this sigh when you realize that your eight-year-old used two bottles of syrup on three toaster waffles before you got up to begin appropriate parental supervision. Of course, every spouse has heard the angry sigh. The air is forced from the lungs with a high degree of intentionality with eyes dilated and brow furrowed. I got this one the other day when I volunteered my wife to provide food for our small group without telling her until the night before. And yes, I ended up with the job. It serves me right. It's the *I-didn't-sign-up-for-this* sigh. You could call it the *sigh's the limit* sigh. An exasperated sigh paints a thousand words, and in many cases, it is followed by a thousand words.

There are many other sighs in the lexicon of nonverbal reactions:

- The *I guess we're going to have to do that again* sigh
- The *I never thought that was going to happen* sigh
- The *I guess the Lions will miss the Super Bowl for the fifty-third straight year* sigh
- The *Diane's kids are so much more civilized than mine* sigh
- The *that's disgusting! why did you eat that?* sigh

Glory Be Declaration

"The life of every living thing is in his hand, as well as the breath of all humanity."

(Job 12:10)

But I do have a favorite sigh. It's the sigh you can enjoy at the end of a good day when, despite all the odds, you realized that God rescued you from every worst-case scenario and close call. You realize that, in the broad scheme of things, life is richer than you could ever imagine because God has walked every circuitous, meandering step with you. That's the sigh where you breathe in a deep breath of His presence and exhale slowly in the safety of His providence. You sigh because His presence was everything you really needed to make your relationships work. In short, that's the sigh of contentment. When we're focused on Jesus, it's the sigh we can practice at the end of every crazy day.

Matt Tullos

Just Thought I'd Ask

I've just finished studying Joseph (the Old Testament one). It is an amazing story that fills most of the back half of the book of Genesis and could be made into a TV movie or a musical or even an animated cartoon. Wait, I think they did all three. The Old Testament is filled with those kinds of stories, and I don't know how heaven will work, but I have lots of questions for Joseph and a few other Old Testament buddies. After "we've been there ten thousand years," I'm bound to run into these guys. Here are a few questions I'd ask today:

Hey, Joseph!

Did you ever get paranoid? Sure, you were the quintessential baby, the family brat. Sure, you were given the power to interpret dreams. Sure, you got the coat of many colors. But this whole life of yours was a universal sting operation until the very end. Did you ever feel like screaming, "My life is full of jerks!"? That would be my response had I been you. I would have blown the whistle on the desperate housewife, starved the brothers, burned the stupid coat, and spent thousands of dollars in therapy. But that's just me. I'm just another Matt. You are Joseph the patriarch.

Howdy, Gideon!

Where'd you come up with the fleece idea? Make it dry. Make it wet. Give me a sign. How'd you come up with that? I was just wondering because this fleece thing has taken on a life of its own. Even my wife uses it whenever I want us to make a decision. "I'll throw out a fleece," she'd reply. I'd say, "Forget the fleece." A simple thumbs up/thumbs down will work just fine for me. I wish a fleece would only refer to an apparel worn on a nippy day. Thanks, Gideon. Thanks a lot.

Oh, David!

One question: In the middle of the ordeals—the spear-dodging, scandal-drenched, sword-fighting, king-avoiding, giant-slaying, big-brother-mocking, victory-dancing, people-pleasing, son-rebelling, mighty-men-sending, cave-dwelling, war-managing, wife-grieving days, did you ever long to go back in time to see that bear fall again with one whirl of the sling?

Glory Be Declaration

"And what more can I say? Time is too short for me to tell about Gideon, Barak, Samson, Jephthah, David, Samuel, and the prophets, who by faith conquered kingdoms, administered justice, obtained promises, shut the mouths of lions."

(Hebrews 11:33-34)

If these questions confuse you, go back and read their stories. I promise it will be worth the time, and they're a whole lot more exciting than Masterpiece Theatre.

That Nagging Smart Watch

I finally got around to buying that smart watch. I've waited many years for it—ever since those days as a kid when Knight Rider, Captain Kirk, Dick Tracy, and George Jetson all had one. Sometimes I wonder why it took them so long. But after a few weeks, I think I'm about ready to ditch it and go back to my old 1984 Casio. You see, it's way too demanding. It nags me all the time.

Watch: *Time to move. You've only taken one hundred seventy steps so far.*
Me: *It's 5 a.m.*
Watch: *Check your email. You have thirteen new messages!*
Me: *Twelve of them are spam.*
Watch: *Time to breathe!*
Me: *What have I been doing? What is the one thing I never stop doing? BREATHING.*
Watch: *Looks like you are on a walk outdoors!*
Me: *Now you're just showing off, Sherlock.*

It is a relentless siege of useless information, and it's always judging me.

Watch: *You got a seventy score on your sleep last night. Poor.*
Me: *I'll try harder to control this while I am unconscious.*

If you ever see me rushing around speaking loudly to my wrist, you'll know that I am furiously looking for my phone while talking to somebody on my watch. The usual response from the caller is, "Are you OK? You sound like you're in a well or something."

A bunch of my younger friends who have the same kind of watch invited me to a weekly step competition. All the alerts have ramped up:

Boogidy Boo is at your heels with six thousand steps. Get some steps in now!
Dudearonomy has overtaken you!

The other day, my dear Darlene caught me walking in place while standing at the refrigerator. She questioned whether that was cheating or not. I don't know. I really don't. I'd love to find a watch app that is more useful as a life coach. It could say,

> *Sounds like your wife needs a little encouragement. Compliment her outfit.*
>
> *Have you prayed today? You sound a bit testy.*
>
> *You haven't opened your Bible in two days. Take ten minutes. Your spirit is running low on food.*

Or,

> *That movie! Turn it off immediately! There's a scene you won't be able to unsee!*

That would be an awesome watch. In truth, there's already an app for that. No purchase necessary. Totally free. It's the Holy Spirit.

Aha Moment

"As for you, the anointing you received from him remains in you, and you don't need anyone to teach you. Instead, his anointing teaches you about all things and is true and is not a lie; just as it has taught you, remain in him."

(1 John 2:27)

Oh-no, Aha, and Glory Be

Matt Tullos

The Oldest Christmas Tradition

If someone asked you about Christmas traditions, you might talk about the Christmas tree, carols, the mistletoe, the nativity scene on the mantle, or Aunt Bertha's fruitcake that has been passed back and forth in the family throughout several international conflicts and four presidential terms. But the oldest tradition of Christmas is *the trip*.

The trip actually started with Mary on a donkey and Joseph dutifully walking beside her holding the reigns. At least that's always been the image we've seen on greeting cards and in church musicals.

For us, it was a six-hundred-mile Christmas sojourn in a minivan with six bladders that constantly demanded attention. I was kind of a *one-stop-every-two-hundred-miles* guy before I got married. But things change with a wife and kids. We learned to drive at night because of the traffic and the chance that the boys would fall asleep and we could listen to music that didn't have anything to do with dinosaurs, old farmers with various animals, or John Jacob Jingleheimer Schmidt. Those songs stick to your brain like gum under the pew.

Back then, we couldn't afford to fly to the grandparents, but it had its advantages. We didn't have to worry about our kids saying something inappropriate to the TSA agents during the walk-through security check. Also, we didn't have to wear the cloak of shame when our kids acted out in front of the more dignified passengers in adjacent seats. In the minivan, we'd just buckle 'em up and let them kick, cry, and laugh as loud and as much as they wanted to. *Just get there.* That was our motto. *Just get there....*

But Mary and Joseph's trip was far more difficult than our interstate odyssey. There's no cruise control on a donkey and no online booking for the Best Eastern Inn in Bethlehem. They didn't even stay at the Best Eastern. They had to stay in the parking garage which, back then, meant the stable. The stable was also the labor room, and a band of country shepherds were the only doctors making the rounds that night.

Christmas reminds me that you can have everything go wrong on a trip and still be in the center of God's plan. It also reminds me of what family is all about. When you're married with kids, you begin an imperfect journey of love and grace. No matter the mess, it's worth celebrating. It's a spiritual journey toward heaven. But hopefully not in a minivan.

Oh-No Admonition

"So he got up, took the child and his mother during the night, and escaped to Egypt."

(Matthew 2:14)

Oh-No, Aha, and Glory Be

Roughing It with the Guys

I voluntarily surrender my man card.

I recently went on a men's retreat with the guys at my church. When I signed up, I thought it was one of those events with Wi-Fi, air conditioning, video-guided Bible study, and all-you-can-eat catfish. But no. A week later, I discovered that I had signed up for sleeping in tents, Coleman lanterns, and brushing my teeth with rainwater. I was out of my element. I'm kind of private; this weekend would be explicitly *not* private. These guys were hard core. We went so far off the grid that the bars disappeared on our phones, and we could hear unknown animals in the distance that sounded like Bigfoot bemoaning a stomach bug. He wasn't far away. I'm sure of that.

Getting off the grid reminded me of what it must have been like to be one of those first disciples. From everything that I've read, being a disciple was like a three-year men's retreat with lots of learning activities. They ate raw wheat straight off the stalks and cooked fish under the stars. Their Leader had no place to lay His head. I doubt the disciples did either. They went on some three-hour tours on rustic boats, and yes, sometimes the weather started getting rough, and their tiny ship was tossed. Team-building exercises included driving out demons, hosting all-you-can-eat buffets for thousands, and water-walking trust exercises.

I came away from those three days realizing that I *needed* to get off the grid. A constant barrage of social media, the twenty-four-hour news cycle, climate-controlled workspaces, and fast food numbs the soul. On the retreat, we didn't text each other funny memes; discuss the stock market or our favorite retro-hip coffee shops; or debate politics, movies, or the implementation of the designated hitter. All those things seemed half a world away. Guys being guys, most of us didn't really plan very well. Only one of us thought to bring toilet paper, which caused the same anxiety we had felt from the recent pandemic.

Strangely, all six of us had moments where we got emotional because we talked about the important stuff, like the way we'd failed as dads, the struggles we faced in our marriages, and our fears about our own mortality. It was holy ground as we prayed, swatted away the flies, and enjoyed an extra-large pot of beanie-weenies over an open fire and washed it down with lukewarm generic-brand root beer. I came away realizing how much I take for granted in my first-world, cushy life and how much my soul craved a stronger connection with brothers and with Jesus. I wouldn't trade the memory of eating half-burned beanie-weenies with a bunch of real friends for *any* climate controlled, humdrum weekend of ease. But next time, I'm remembering the toilet paper.

Glory Be Declaration

"But ask the animals, and they will instruct you; ask the birds of the sky, and they will tell you. Or speak to the earth, and it will instruct you; let the fish of the sea inform you. Which of all these does not know that the hand of the Lord has done this? The life of every living thing is in his hand, as well as the breath of all humanity."

(Job 12:7-10)

Oh-No, Aha, and Glory Be

The Basement Tour

While cleaning out the basement, I've seen things I've not seen in a number of months, even years. My tendency is to be a thrower away of stuff. This leads to lots of family bargaining.

Everyone in the house gets a tad nervous when I go down to the basement to organize. Over the past few years, they've effectively trained me to get approval.

Our basement has helmets for football players whose draft possibilities have long since passed. We have old books that have been conveniently replaced by iPads. My wife still has her pom-poms from cheerleading in high school. They've lost their luster, but we can't seem to get rid of them. We've got awards, skateboards, typewriters, baby shoes, microwaves, coffee cans of nails, lava lamps (first generation), video tapes, rollerblades of all sizes, and video games (the ones that work if you blow on them). Most items have traveled in the same box from New Orleans to Amarillo and three different homes in Nashville. Yes, it's embarrassing. We've got overalls, flare jeans, ballroom dresses, and lots of bubble wrapped sacred artifacts.

But this spring we will do it. We'll have a garage sale, the scope of which will rival any large discount store. And we might make upwards of one hundred dollars!

It's uncanny how often I see couples like us—an accumulator married to a discarder.

As I look at the things we have, I'm reminded that we aren't in God's basement. He hasn't placed any of us in a musty box, waiting for our moment to rise to the main floor. GOD USES EVERYTHING. He has not shelved you. He has not pushed you out to the curb, holding a sign which reads, *Free Dude.* You are on the main floor.

The fact that God would choose me to father such amazing sons and be the husband of such a patient, loving wife is astounding to me. Perhaps you have the same thought: *Why does God keep me around these days when I fail more than I succeed?* It's at those moments of epic failure when I remember that the kingdom of God is not a flea market. As rough as we are, God uses everything to weave amazing stories. . . .

The recovering drug addict, the guy who had an awful marriage and worked to make it incredible, the kid who grew up in a dysfunctional family, the person who has a chronic disease, the woman who experienced sexual abuse, the guy who was unemployed for three months, the stutterer, the kid with Down syndrome, the family whose house was robbed while they were on vacation, the former stripper, the couple that faced infertility, the guy who went for help for his addiction to porn, the blind guy, the man who lost his wife, the grandmother who lost connection with her grandchildren, the child of alcoholic parents, the parents of an autistic child, the falsely accused—none of these people are stuffed in a ratty box in God's eternal basement. These are His prized, redeemed possessions! And you and I, wives, husbands, single moms and dads, kids, orphans, young, old, rich, poor . . . we are all invited out of our boxes and basements to be on display as objects of God's great love.

Well, back to the basement. Anyone want an old DC Talk cassette? Hit me up.

Glory Be Declaration

"I remember the days of old; I meditate on all you have done; I reflect on the work of your hands."
(Psalm 143:5)

Lost in the Hills

I recently had an adventure in the backwoods of Kentucky. I was performing a funeral for a lady I pastored around twenty years ago. Somehow, I made an impression on this dear lady. Her son called and said his mom made him promise that I would do her funeral. Martha lived up to her name in the small town where I pastored. Like the Martha in the New Testament, she was a busy soul with some unbelievable culinary skills. After her husband had passed, she moved to Kentucky to be closer to her kids.

Driving to this little village in Kentucky was like driving into a bad episode of the *X-Files*. The closer I got to the destination, the more the apps on my phone became dysfunctional. But my maps app worked just fine and led me directly to the church. After my time in WhereTheHeckAmI, USA, I hopped in the car to head back. I tapped "home" on my maps app, and it stared back at me with a blank expression. My phone had complete amnesia regarding my whereabouts, how I got wherever I was, and how to get back to *any* road that was paved. I don't think Siri™ even knew who I was! I really wasn't paying much attention to where I was going on my drive, and by the time I doubled back to the church for directions, everybody had left. I wondered if I would ever see my wife and children again. Seriously.

I found myself on a country road somewhere in Kentucky where cows and deer far outnumbered humans. And to top it all off, I was almost out of gas. I kept driving around looking for bars (as in cell towers, not margaritas . . . just to be clear). Finally, I came across an intersection. A real intersection! I saw a stop sign! Hallelujah! I hadn't seen any kind of traffic sign in twenty miles, only a few homemade taxidermy signs offering two deer heads for the price of one. Still no cell service, but I actually saw a couple cars on the road! After a couple of miles, I saw the most glorious sight: a gas station with an actual person behind the cash register. She was able to point me back to the nearest homebound highway. I was never happier to hear my phone light up with fifty or so alerts that finally came through simultaneously. Siri woke up and knew who she was, who I was, and where I lived. All was right in the world again. I was never so thankful to see my wife and son that Saturday night.

Once I got back to civilization, I bought a map book of the entire United States and stuck it in the back seat of my Accord. Sometimes you've just got to go analog. God showed up big time for me last week. If He didn't, I might still be wandering on foot down a winding road ten miles away from Pippa Passes, Kentucky.

Oh-No Admonition

"I know, Lord, that a person's way of life is not his own; no one who walks determines his own steps."
(Jeremiah 10:23)

Matt Tullos

Spooky Phone Conversation Starters

The book of James reminds us repeatedly that words carry great power. "The tongue is a fire. The tongue, a world of unrighteousness, is placed among our members. It stains the whole body, sets the course of life on fire, and is itself set on fire by hell" (James 3:6).

For me, that's pretty darn scary. But there are certain words and phrases at the beginning of phone calls that give me the shivers when I hear them. Here are my top four that cause me to break out in hives.

1. "God gave me a word for you." So, God has a word for me, and you are going to tell me that word? I am petrified. Not because I am afraid of hearing from God . . . I talk to Him every day. But getting a word from God vicariously from another guy? Yikes! How did He tell you? Was it a dream influenced by cold pizza the night before? Is this going to be embarrassing? Why'd He tell you? Now I can vouch that some brothers have had a real word from God for me, but usually when someone says that, they've got something they want me to do, or they want me to change a decision I've made that involves them.
2. "I've got some good news, and I've got some bad news." I'm slightly panicked, and don't ask me which one I want to hear first. Give me the bad news. I'm Southern Baptist for goodness' sake.
3. "First, let me say, everybody's OK." When my wife or kids say this, I know whatever happened is going to be very expensive, but nobody lost a limb. Just tell me the story, and we'll figure it all out as soon as this hyperventilation I am experiencing subsides.
4. "Just chill, I got this." I am both mortified and slightly amused. This is man-speak for *I am going to fake it 'til I make it*. It usually involves feats of daring in the midst of a doomed, ill-fated plan soon to become a cautionary tale. My sons love this, especially when they don't want their father's advice. When someone says, "Just chill. I got this," usually something entertaining and a little scary is about to happen. However, it's my favorite paraphrase of, "Be still and know that I am God." I want God to say that once a day and twice on Sunday.

These are my least favorite spooky phone phrases. They're almost as scary as the time my doctor said, "Ew!" during my annual physical.

Oh-No Admonition

"Now if we put bits into the mouths of horses so that they obey us, we direct their whole bodies. And consider ships: Though very large and driven by fierce winds, they are guided by a very small rudder wherever the will of the pilot directs. So too, though the tongue is a small part of the body, it boasts great things. Consider how a small fire sets ablaze a large forest."

(James 3:3-5)

Oh-No, Aha, and Glory Be

One Man's Treasure

Well, it happened. My car got broken into last week. Actually it didn't get broken into because I forgot to lock it up before I went to bed. The next morning my neighbor called and said he found my expired gas card in his lawn. I went outside and saw the door wide open and under it a pile of rejected merchandise. Obviously, there was a lot of riffling that went on in my car. I'm not super clean with my 2012 Accord, but this bandit definitely made things worse. I went back and reviewed my door cam. As I witnessed the carnage of his 2 a.m. siege on my super cool 2012 Accord, I was perplexed. There was so much good stuff he could have taken. He left behind copies of three small group studies; one was even written by Rick Warren. Sorry, Rick, he wasn't interested. He found one of my favorite Bibles that I always keep in my car as a spare, just in case I head out to my men's breakfast/Bible study and forget my regular Bible.

He totally missed that it was genuine cowhide leather. I had several CDs that were vintage recordings of Christian 80s heavy metal. I paid a lot for them because they were autographed and, in my opinion, quite a treasure. My car doesn't do Bluetooth, so there's that. The guy just pulled them out and tossed them in the back seat like yesterday's news. Evidently this was the worst heist he had ever pulled off. All he ended up with was a flashlight that I probably paid three dollars for ten years ago. But I really liked it, and I'll miss it. The one thing that was obvious as he finished his great siege was his frustration. Even though he was wearing a hoody, I could tell that he was shaking his head in disgust as he exited the car. I'm reminded that one man's treasure is another man's trash. And I'm totally OK with that.

Oh-No Admonition

"Don't store up for yourselves treasures on earth, where moth and rust destroy and where thieves break in and steal. But store up for yourselves treasures in heaven, where neither moth nor rust destroys, and where thieves don't break in and steal. For where your treasure is, there your heart will be also."

(Matthew 6:19-21)

Matt Tullos

The Mystery of "Eeeev-body"

Christmas is a time of mystery. It's when we ponder the transcendent questions like prophecy, the virgin birth, incarnation, and the shelf life of fruitcake. Most of us can quote the story along with Linus every Christmas. It's mysterious and poetic. But the mortals in the narrative were just ordinary people, not theologians, royalty, or intellectuals. It's a blue collar tale on an ordinary night until glory came a-crashing through. The mystery, wonder, and glory fell right into laps of shepherds. They were the country bumpkins of Bethlehem. They were just working the night shift, swapping stories and watching over the dumbest, most helpless animals in God's creation.

The Magi had their dreams, but the shepherds were wide awake staring straight into the eyes of divine glory. *They were sore afraid.* In other words, scared out of their cloaks. They heard it first, not the innkeepers, rulers, and big shots. God chose the lower-class grunts of society to get the news first, and, yes, they were mortified. I can just see one of them falling to his knees, begging God in broken Hebrew, *Jehovah, forgive me for breakin' the Sabbath two weeks ago. Forgive me for eating that bacon when I was in Samaria! And for yelling at my wife last Thursday. And for sleeping on the job!*

The lights, an angelic announcement, the clamor, the stunned sheep! And then a voice that would make James Earl Jones sound like a preadolescent middle schooler speaks from the heavenlies:

"Don't be afraid! I bring you good news of great joy which shall be to all people." What a relief! This was good news for everybody! It reminds me of those Christmas mornings when our four boys were still very young. There'd always be some gift marked for all of them. Nathan, our four-year-old, would guard it, waving his little hands and announcing to the other three, "No, no, no, no! This fo' eeeev-body." He couldn't articulate the word, but he wanted us all to know that this package wasn't just for his older brothers. "It's fo' eeeev-body."

I'm so glad that the gospel is for everybody. I think that's why God went first to shepherds with little money and no deodorant and void of the social grace. God scanned the earth. He saw the powerful, the rich, the literate, the graceful, the independent, the philosophical, and the artistic. He pondered the announcement and decided that those random shepherds would do just fine. He came to them. And He came to me. And that's why they call it good news. It's fo' eeeev-body!

Glory Be Declaration

"Then an angel of the Lord stood before them, and the glory of the Lord shone around them, and they were terrified. But the angel said to them, 'Don't be afraid, for look, I proclaim to you good news of great joy that will be for all the people.'"

(Luke 2:9-10)

The Final Glory Be!

I am constantly amazed by the faithful love of Jesus. He champions the threshold of my beginnings and endings. He initiated the relationship and never lets go. I am still overwhelmed, surprised, and consumed by His love. He is trustworthy when I am sick. When I struggle with sin, He refuses to write me off. He is the friend of sinners.

He is faithfully consistent. Truly, there is no shifting shadow in the deep love of Jesus. When I cast my gaze across the horizon—the October breeze that refreshes the land after the long summer—I know that every falling leaf, every blade of grass, and every bird and cloud is a reminder of His creative hand. They all were conceived first in the imagination of the Artisan of the cosmos.

And as I reflect on the life I've lived here, mostly fearful of everything, I realize that I never, *ever* had anything to fear. He has been and always will be relentlessly faithful, continuously sufficient, and absolutely available. I am still captivated by this lowly carpenter and faithful Redeemer—I'm still struggling awkwardly to construct the right syntax and composition of words to describe the One who is truly indescribable. I will continue to try until the book is closed and my time comes.

King Jesus, Your presence is palpable, and Your depth is dependable.

Matt Tullos

The Big Story

We were born with a deep sense of eternity. It's inside us. It echoes through our doubts and struggles for meaning and hope. But we must ask, *Is this life really all there is?*

We are shaped and formed by a living God! There's too much beauty, too much wonder, too much extravagance for a simplistic, crude explanation that everything around us is merely accidental. Just a meaningless, "Oh-No." Like pottery in His hands, He crafted the world in all its beauty and symmetry. It's a portrait of a present and active God, lovingly desiring to connect with His creation. Through wars, chaos, injustice, and disease, He's been reaching out.

Oh-No! There's a BIG problem!

The problem is that the bridge was broken between the Creator and His creation.

Aha! God loves us!

The Bible also writes that God's perfect Son was born and lived a perfect life. Jesus showed us how to live, and then He died as a sacrifice for our sins. God so loved the world, that He gave His one and only Son, that whoever believes in His Son, Jesus, will not die, but have eternal life. How did He prove His divine nature? He did what no other person ever did. He died and was resurrected, never to die again. What we've earned is death.

But the gift God gives to those who believe is eternal life. It's not religion. It's not legalism. It's not performance. It's grace. This gift of grace and eternal life is yours when you lay down your life and trust in the power of God to forgive you of your sins and to bring you to the table of His loving family. What do you have to lose if you refuse this gift?

EVERYTHING.

So would you pray this prayer and join the movement of God that began so long ago?

Father God, I am in need of forgiveness and belonging. I believe that Your Son came into this world, lived a perfect life, and paid the death penalty for my sin. I accept the gift of being part of Your family. Thank You for the eternal life You offer. I lay everything down at Your feet. Forgive me, wash me clean, and take me. I'm Yours.

If you've prayed that prayer, we want to welcome you to a family.

Glory Be!

That's the big story. God is greater that all the *Oh-Nos* you'll encounter. May He provide many *Ahas* in the days ahead. And may we all be in a constant state of *Glory Be*.

Finally, I'd love to hear your story, whether it's an *Oh-No*, *Aha*, or *Glory Be*!

Acknowledgments

Special thanks and acknowledgement to...

Darlene, Isaac, Jacob, Nathan, and Caleb, for providing so much material and so many memories! You are my personal miracles.

My brother and sisters, Mark, Melodye, and Melinda, three of the best people in the world.

Mike Salva, for providing artistic tweaks and a really cool lightbulb!

David Bennet and Tann Flippen, editors at Homelife and Stand Firm.

Dr. Randy C. Davis, best leader I've ever known.

And finally, Rachael Carrington, Yvonne Parks, and Dr. Bart Dahmer at Innovo Publishing, for their efforts to make this little ten-year-old idea a reality.

www.ingramcontent.com/pod-product-compliance
Lightning Source LLC
Chambersburg PA
CBHW081232170426
43198CB00017B/2739